family
fun in
Yellowstone
National Park

Robin Tawney

FALCON®

A FALCON GUIDE ®

Falcon® is continually expanding its list of recreational guidebooks. All books include detailed descriptions, accurate maps, and all the information necessary for enjoyable trips. You can order extra copies of this book and get information and prices for other Falcon® guidebooks by writing The Globe Pequot Press, P.O. Box 480, Guilford, Connecticut, 06437 or calling toll-free 1-800-582-2665. Also, please ask for a free copy of our current catalog. Visit our website at www.falcon.com or contact us by e-mail at falcon@falcon.com.

1 2 3 4 5 6 7 8 9 0 MG 06 05 04 03 02 01

Falcon and FalconGuide are registered trademarks of Falcon® Publishing, Inc.

Cover photos: family on boardwalk by Fred Pflughoft.
All other cover photos by Mike Sample.
Text photos by author, unless noted otherwise.
Illustrations by Susan Carlson.

Cataloging-in-Publication Data is on file at the Library of Congress.

CAUTION

All participants in the recreational activities suggested by this book must assume responsibility for their own actions and safety. The information contained in this guidebook cannot replace sound judgment and good decision-making skills, which help reduce risk exposure, nor does the scope of this book allow for disclosure of all the potential hazards and risks involved in such activities.

Learn as much as possible about the recreational activities in which you participate, prepare for the unexpected, and be cautious. The reward will be a safer and more enjoyable experience.

 Text pages printed on recycled paper.

Contents

. . . .

YELLOWSTONE NATIONAL PARK

· · · · · · · · · · · · · · · · · ·

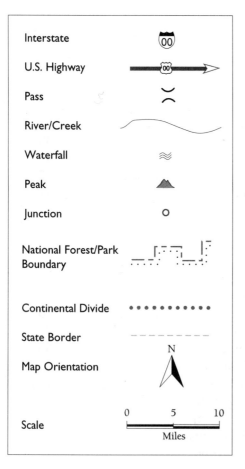

Interstate	00
U.S. Highway	00 →
Pass	‿
River/Creek	～
Waterfall	≈
Peak	▲
Junction	○
National Forest/Park Boundary	
Continental Divide	• • • • • • • • • •
State Border	– – – – –
Map Orientation	N ▲
Scale	0 5 10 Miles

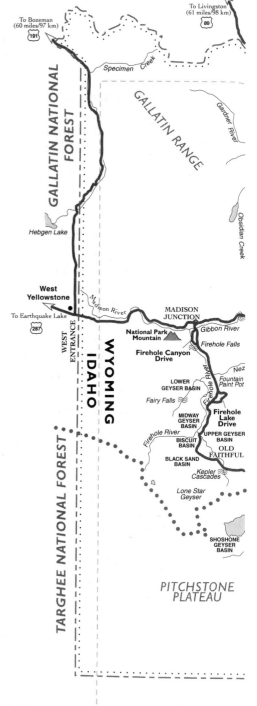

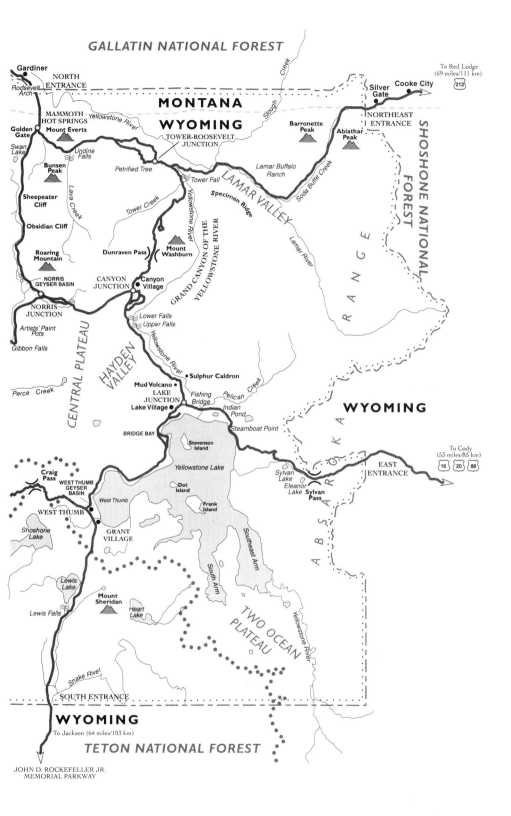

To the memory of Leonard and Sandy Sargent,
caretakers and caregivers of the natural resources and
the people of the Greater Yellowstone Ecosystem

PREFACE

Yellowstone and I share a birthday—March 1. Perhaps that is why I am so fascinated by this park, but I doubt it. No, I am in awe of its beauty, its starkness, its wildness, its dynamic nature. Yellowstone calls to me always.

Much has happened in the 13 years since I first wrote a children's guide to Yellowstone National Park. The park has seen significant changes: the fires of 1988, the 1995 reintroduction of the wolf, and current far-reaching thermophilic research. These changes have been coupled with challenges, including the serious boundary issues regarding bison and elk winter migrations and the threat of mining near the park border. These years have also seen great changes in my personal life: the birth of my third child, Whitney, and the death of my husband, Philip. My oldest children, Land and Mikal, shared my earlier explorations and are now midway through college. Through it all, Yellowstone has remained a touchstone—a reminder that wildness is essential to life on this planet, and that change is the nature of all things.

I embarked on this version of my original *Young People's Guide to Yellowstone National Park* with great humbleness. I conclude my work with continued awe and respect for one remarkable piece of real estate and the people who tend it.

This time around I had the companionship and on-site research assistance of Whitney and my partner William Nichols. I thank them both for their love, patience, and insight. My dad, Robert Brown, once again meticulously proofed my manuscript, and my mother, Cidney Brown, provided essential, unconditional support. Beth Kaeding, public affairs specialist with the National Park Service, volunteered her invaluable service as fact-checker— a tough job, since Yellowstone is an ever-changing place. Other Park Service professionals who provided me assistance and inspiration include: Norman Bishop, retired natural resource specialist; Ginny Cowan, publications specialist; Marsha Karle, public affairs officer; Cheryl Matthews, public affairs assistant; Terry McEneaney, ornithologist; Roy Renkin, management biologist; John Sacklin, planner; Doug Smith, wolf biologist; Ron Thoman, former chief of interpretation and current regional chief of interpretation; Ellen Petrick-Underwood, environmental education program coordinator; John Varley, chief of research; and Linda Young, acting chief of interpretation. Special thanks also go to Mary Flaming, who recently retired from the Yellowstone Association, for her encouragement, as well as to my dear family and friends who have born my absence from activities with care and understanding.

Along Obsidian Creek are what I call "infant" hot springs. In the major geyser basins, these tiny, bubbly pools might easily be overlooked.

One day as I sat quietly watching a round white pebble in its endless dance over the vent of one of these precious pools, I was reminded of something the late Wallace Stegner wrote about public lands. He called them "a safety valve of the spirit." And so Yellowstone is for me—a place to contemplate the small as well as the grand, and, in doing so, I become renewed.

Robin Tawney
April 1998

welcome to
YELLOWSTONE NATIONAL PARK

. . . .

Yellowstone. The very name conjures up images of geysers, bears, hot pots, bison, and open, wild country. It is the stuff of dreams and of a wonderful reality that beckons you to investigate.

With 10,000 geysers and hot springs—more than the rest of the world put together—Yellowstone National Park is a place of superlatives. The world's first national park and the largest intact temperate ecosystem in the world, Yellowstone is still home to every animal species that was present here in pre-Columbian times, including North America's largest and fastest land animals (the bison and the pronghorn antelope), the world's largest member of the deer family (the moose), two endangered species (the gray wolf and the whooping crane), and three threatened species (the grizzly bear, the lynx, and the bald eagle). All of these animals and more continue to live in a wild state because Yellowstone's more than 3 million annual human visitors are concentrated in only 2 percent of the park's 3,472 square miles (or 5,555 km², which is about 2.2 million acres or 900,000 hectares).

Larger than the states of Rhode Island and Delaware combined, Yellowstone is tucked into the northwestern corner of Wyoming, easing over slightly into Montana and Idaho. The park straddles the Continental Divide, the backbone of the northern Rocky Mountains. Most of it lies 7,000 to 9,000 feet (2,100–2,700 m) above sea level, though elevations range from 5,282 feet (1,585 m) at Reese Creek near the park's North Entrance to 11,358 feet (3,463 m) at the summit of Eagle Peak on the park's southeastern boundary.

Designated a Biosphere Reserve by the United Nations (UN) in 1976, Yellowstone joined an international network of protected samples of the world's major ecosystem types "devoted to conservation of nature and scientific research in the service of man." This network, according to the UN proclamation, "provides a standard against which the effect of man's impact on the environment can be measured."

In 1978, the UN recognized Yellowstone as a World Heritage Site, one of a select number of "protected areas around the world whose outstanding natural and cultural resources form the common inheritance of all mankind."

Managing this "common inheritance" is a complex task. Since Yellowstone's establishment in 1872, park officials have grappled with a variety of tough management issues; this book will touch on some of them. In many cases, the issues have extended beyond the borders of the park and have required the cooperative effort of the National Park Service and other federal and state government agencies.

If you have never been to Yellowstone, you are in for a special treat. If this is your second, third, or fourth trip, you may be surprised at the changes you find. Some features may even change during your visit. So keep track of what you see by jotting notes and drawing sketches in the margins of this book. Have everyone in your family or group keep a journal to document your "Yellowstone days."

Winter: The Other Season (mid-December to early March)

A vast and quiet landscape resting under a thick blanket of snow; steamy thermal plumes billowing to meet a brilliant blue sky; bison and elk congregating in geyser basins to absorb warmth from the heated earth. These images have attracted a growing number of cross-country skiers and snowmobilers to the park each year.

Winter visitor numbers burgeoned from 56,432 in the winter of 1976–1977 to a high of 143,523 in 1993–1994. The greater number of winter visitors has caused concern about overcrowding, noise and air pollution from snowmobiles, non-availability of facilities, and visitor impact on natural resources. Since winter-visitor use in Yellowstone is a relatively new phenomenon, these issues have come up fairly recently, but the dilemma they point to is as old as the park itself.

The original mandate of the National Park Service, which still stands, is "to conserve the scenery and the natural and historic objects and the wild life therein and to provide for the enjoyment of the same in such a manner and by such means as will leave them unimpaired for the enjoyment of future generations." Yellowstone National Park must serve two masters: preservation and human pleasure.

At the time of this writing, an interagency team is preparing a winter-use management plan for Yellowstone and Grand Teton national parks and seven adjacent national forests. The plan will aim to protect natural resources while providing quality visitor experiences. Whatever the team's recommendations, they will be made with the Park Service mandate in mind.

A National Park is Born

To hear mountain man Jim Bridger tell it, Yellowstone was an enchanted place. Around campfires in the 1830s, Bridger spun yarns about glass mountains you could see right through and petrified birds perched on petrified trees singing petrified songs in which every note turned to stone. He claimed this paradise was plumb full of fur-bearers and other wildlife, too, but here he was a bit closer to the truth.

Even as the last Ice Age began to wane, more than 10,000 years ago, the first visitors to Yellowstone found a land of plenty. They came to the area to hunt the giant bison and other game that foraged in abundance, and to harvest berries, seeds, and roots. As the climate warmed, these nomadic hunters and gatherers began staying longer in Yellowstone, leaving remnants of their ancient seasonal campsites throughout the park—projectile points, stone tools, and domestic utensils, among other things.

In the late 1600s, the introduction of the modern horse gave people new mobility; in many cases, it forever changed their tribal cultures. On horseback, Native Americans could follow the migrations of the vast herds of bison and other game across the plains. The Absarokas, or Crows, settled to the east of the park, the Blackfeet to the north, and the Shoshone Bannocks to the northwest. After that, the Crows and Blackfeet sent only occasional hunting parties into Yellowstone. Some Bannocks may have visited annually in search of their winter's meat.

A few small bands of horseless Shoshone Bannocks are the only Indians known to have lived year-round in the park. Called Sheepeaters because they subsisted on bighorn sheep, they made bows for hunting by soaking the curved sheep horns in the park's hot springs to straighten them. Archaeological evidence shows that other Native Americans also frequented the geyser basins, debunking a long-held myth that these early people feared the geysers and avoided them.

In the late 1700s, EuroAmerican fur trappers followed the largest tributary of the Missouri River west in search of beaver. Mostly French Canadians, these mountain men called this tributary "Roche Jaune," or "Rock Yellow," because of the yellow rock that lined the banks of its lower reaches. We call this river "Yellowstone." Apparently, none of these men ever saw the natural wonders upstream.

Geysers, hot springs, and spectacular waterfalls were not on the agenda of the Corps of Discovery either. President Thomas Jefferson sent Meriwether Lewis and William Clark and their corps west in 1804–1806 to find an all-water route to the Pacific (allowing for brief passage over the Rocky Mountains) and to seek new opportunities for trade. On their homeward journey, Lewis and Clark extended their exploration for a time by pursuing separate routes. Clark passed just 56 miles (90 km) north of what would later become Yellowstone National Park. In their journals neither Lewis nor Clark even mentions rumors about the region's hot-water phenomena; they had heard reports only about Yellowstone Lake.

One of the members of the Lewis and Clark Expedition eventually became the first white man known to see the area's geysers and hot springs. Near the end of the expedition, John Colter asked for permission to leave and headed back into the wilds to trap beaver. The next year, Colter hired on with a Yellowstone River trading post and spent 1807–1808 exploring the region. He returned from this venture with tales of explosive geysers, towering waterfalls, a gigantic lake, and an unlimited fur supply.

Yellowstone was immediately dubbed "Colter's Hell," although historians have since shown that the colorful fur trader did not visit the geyser basins and probably passed north of Yellowstone Lake. Through careful research, the true "Colter's Hell" has been identified as DeMaris Springs, near what is now Cody, Wyoming.

Rumors about the Yellowstone area persisted. In the 1820s, mountain men like Jim Bridger, Jedediah Smith, and Daniel Potts headed west, where they saw what Yellowstone had to offer, and began to spin their own outrageous yarns. Their tall tales eventually reached more "civilized" parts, piquing the curiosity of Main Street, U.S.A.

Expeditions to Yellowstone

By 1840, the mountain men had trapped most of the West's beavers. The subsequent lack of beaver pelts and a change in fashion in the East from beaver hats to black silk hats abruptly ended the fur trade. For the next 20 years, white men left Yellowstone to the resident Sheepeater Indians and to seasonal Indian hunters.

Then, in 1862, gold was discovered in Montana. Prospectors flocked to Yellowstone the following year, but this time the explorers were out of luck. Despite an intense search of nearly every inch of what would become the park, the would-be miners could not find gold. They did, however, spark new interest in the other features of this wondrous land. Countless eyewitness stories and a map drawn by prospector-cum-surveyor Walter W. DeLacy brought three important exploring parties to Yellowstone country between 1869 and 1871.

The first party, organized in 1869, was nearly aborted because of rumors of Indian trouble. When a military escort failed to materialize, only three explorers had the courage to proceed: David Folsom, Charles W. Cook, and William Peterson. They pressed onward, meeting few Indians—none of them hostile—and returned with news about incredible phenomena that fueled the growing national curiosity. Folsom collaborated with prospector DeLacy on a better map and wrote an article for *Western Monthly* magazine under Cook's byline.

The next year, despite more talk about Indian trouble, several of Montana Territory's leading politicians and businessmen organized another exploration. Surveyor General Henry D. Washburn led the party, which had a military escort headed by Lieutenant Gustavus C. Doane, commander of the Second Cavalry. They began their journey as skeptics and ended it as true believers.

The influential men of the Washburn-Langford-Doane expedition would settle for nothing less than the establishment of Yellowstone as the world's first national park. Politician and promoter Nathaniel Langford lectured and wrote a widely read series of articles about the area for *Scribner's Monthly*. Lieutenant Doane produced an official report of the 1870 expedition for the U.S. Congress, and others in the party wrote numerous newspaper articles, all advocating preservation.

The Northern Pacific Railroad Company added to the frenzy, exalting Yellowstone's

The Yellowstone Park Act

Be it enacted by the Senate and House of Representatives of the United States of America in Congress assembled, That the tract of land in the Territories of Montana and Wyoming lying near the headwaters of the Yellowstone river . . . is hereby reserved and withdrawn from settlement, occupancy, or sale under the laws of the United States, and dedicated and set apart as a public park or pleasureing [sic] ground for the benefit and enjoyment of the people. . . .

wonders to attract customers for its new rail service to the West Coast. In 1871, capitalizing on what would surely become a major vacation destination, an agent for the Northern Pacific suggested: "Let Congress pass a bill reserving the Great Geyser Basin as a public park forever."

Still healing from the Civil War, the nation was in need of a positive diversion. Congress welcomed the boosterism and appropriated funds for an official scientific exploration of Yellowstone, appointing Ferdinand V. Hayden, territorial director of the U.S. Geological Survey, to lead the expedition. The results of the 1871 survey verified the reports of earlier explorers. Hayden joined the illustrious members of the Washburn party in lobbying Congress. He brought to life their collective appeal with photographs, paintings, and sketches.

Washburn, Langford, Hayden, and others worked feverishly to expand on a precedent Congress had set in 1864, when it reserved a piece of wilderness in California. At that time, the Louisiana Purchase had given the United States jurisdiction over the western half of the Mississippi River drainage. Congress recognized the unique natural setting of the Yosemite Valley and gave the state of California lands surrounding the valley to hold settlement at bay "upon the express conditions that the premises shall be held for public use, resort, and recreation" and "shall be inalienable for all time."

The public gave Yellowstone overwhelming support. Unlike almost any other proposal that has ever gone before Congress, the bill establishing Yellowstone National Park was passed with little debate. On March 1, 1872, President Ulysses S. Grant signed the Yellowstone Park Act into law.

The Early Years of Yellowstone National Park

The act establishing Yellowstone as a national park was proposed, adopted by both houses of Congress, and signed by the President with a head-spinning speed that was altogether necessary. The very idea ran full-tilt against the general direction of popular culture. Although Henry David Thoreau and other naturalist philosophers had developed and expounded upon the tenets of conservation, the federal government's Homestead Act of 1864 and other legislation had offered the frontier and all of its bountifulness to free-wheeling development.

The government also deeded millions of acres to the railroads to open up the West. To make room for rail lines and white settlement, bison were killed by the thousands, and the Plains Indians, who were dependent on the shaggy beasts for their food and clothing, were moved from their ancestral homelands. Lumbermen leveled millions of acres of timber in cold and arid reaches without considering whether reforestation was even possible. Cattlemen grazing their vast herds left bare soil where tall prairie grasses had grown and moved on to greener pastures.

Somehow, despite this rush to develop the West, Yellowstone was singled out. Yet the irony of Yellowstone's creation is that, while the people overwhelmingly agreed that it must be preserved, the first park tourists epitomized the frontier mentality. They arrived armed with shovels and axes to hack, pry up, and haul away ancient pieces of geyserite and travertine. When they weren't souvenir-hunting, the tourists were probing the depths of the hot springs with logs or lobbing anything they could find into the geysers to watch their water-soaked missiles rocket skyward. The hunters among them slaughtered Yellowstone's elk and deer, often taking with them only trophy antlers, hides, and, in the case of elk, ivory teeth.

Soon after the establishment of the National Park Service, a ranger patrols along the Firehole River, using a single pole with his long wooden skis. Photo courtesy of National Park Service

The attitudes and behavior of Yellowstone's first tourists pointed out a near-fatal flaw in the hasty drafting and passage of the bill establishing the park. The framers of this landmark legislation naively assumed that the people's park could be managed without any cost to the people. They believed fees charged to concessioners would pay for road building, maintenance, and protection of resources from poaching and vandalism. Therefore, the act that established Yellowstone National Park provided no funding—period. Even the park's first superintendent, Nathaniel P. Langford of the 1870 Washburn party, served without pay.

The government quickly learned a hard lesson: millions of acres cannot be managed on goodwill alone. The new park was still an almost impassable wilderness, making access and a profitable tourist trade nearly impossible. The closest railroad was still 500 miles (800 km) away, and good roads and bridges were only pipe dreams. Yet hardy pioneer tourists still came to see their national legacy and haul bits of it away. A growing parade of concessioners did little or nothing to ensure the preservation and protection of the new park.

Politics and Yellowstone's isolation continued to work to the park's disadvantage. The second superintendent, P. W. Norris, finally received funding in 1877. During his five-year tenure, he campaigned to stop poachers and vandals, laid out and built the park's first road system, and constantly studied and explored Yellowstone, naming many of its features. The park still had primitive roads and lacked proper accommodations, but each year an increasing number of hardy tourists bumped through on wagons or horseback. They soaked in hot pools and slept in the crude "hotels" and camps offered by concessioners. And they continued to take genuine Yellowstone souvenirs home with them.

Even the threat of Indian trouble caused the early tourists little hesitation in their eagerness to see the park. In 1877, two groups of ten tourists each were warned that 700 Nez Perce were crossing the park to escape capture by the Army and subsequent confinement on a reservation. One party of tourists chose to linger; the other had completed its tour and was homeward bound. Despite the vastness of Yellowstone, trails were already well established and the inevitable happened: the Nez Perce surprised both parties and took several tourists hostage for a short time. Two tourists were killed and four were wounded.

Two months later, the Nez Perce, led by Chief Joseph and several other chiefs, were captured in north-central Montana, just before reaching Canada and freedom. You can read about their sad journey through the eyes of a fast-maturing six-year-old boy in *Soun Tetoken: Nez Perce Boy* by Kenneth Thomasma.

After the flight of the Nez Perce, the threat of Indian trouble was virtually gone and Yellowstone's visitor numbers increased. Concessioners and tourists, some exploitative, some not, continued to set the direction in Yellowstone. By the mid-1880s, the Northern Pacific Railroad reached the park's North Entrance at Gardiner, Montana. Other major railroads built spur lines close to other park entrances, and they all vied for upper-middle-class tourists. Many rail lines offered week-long vacation packages featuring stagecoach tours with stopovers in new luxury hotels near the park's major attractions. They even outfitted visitors with linen dusters to protect woolen suits and floor-sweeping dresses from the elements. Rustic accommodations, in the form of tent camps, attracted adventurous tourists of more modest means. A toll road from Bozeman, Montana, brought some visitors to the West Entrance.

The park administration firmly aligned itself with concessioners. One superintendent even plotted to gain an inholding (privately owned land within a national park) for personal use. And the people kept coming, most taking away more than memories from their visit to Yellowstone National Park.

U.S. Cavalry to the Rescue

At last, after Yellowstone had suffered years of abuse, the government realized something had to be done. In a move approved by Congress, the Secretary of the Interior asked the Secretary of War for help, and in August 1886, the U.S. Cavalry arrived to restore order to Yellowstone.

The Army began its mission by setting up outposts at the park's major attractions and sending out daily patrols to stop poaching and vandalism. As appropriations for the task increased, the soldiers built many of the Fort Yellowstone buildings at Mammoth Hot Springs, current park headquarters. The Army enlisted the Corps of Engineers to replace the park's rough roads and trails with a user-friendly, resource-friendly system that, for the most part, endures today.

Despite a lack of legislative authority, the Army persisted in its protection of all wildlife, setting a precedent for national park management. Nearly all of our national parks today are also wildlife refuges; hunting is allowed in only a few specific National Park Service areas, mainly in Alaska.

The ranger-naturalist program began in the late nineteenth century when the soldiers were ordered to answer visitors' queries about Yellowstone's natural curiosities. In 1908, seeing a need to enhance the soldiers' ability to field these questions, the park's acting superintendent asked the government for books on natural history for the "better education and information" of the protectors of the park.

In 1902, the first automobile to enter the park was evicted. In 1915, the Secretary of the Interior opened Yellowstone to this new mode of transportation. Automobile use was severely restricted at first, and the park required expensive permits; but still the cars came. Concessioners soon replaced stagecoaches with automobile stages, and travel on horseback was relegated to the backcountry. Many of the camps, hotels, and lunch stations that concessioners strategically located for stagecoach travel disappeared. Paved roads, parking areas convenient to scenic attractions, and public campgrounds with fresh water, fuel, and sanitation facilities better served the needs of modern visitors.

The automobile brought democracy to Yellowstone. No longer just a vacation spot for the wealthy or for adventuresome campers, Yellowstone became a truly national park, accessible to anyone who could afford a car. Visitors were free to follow their own schedules, unhampered by the itineraries of concessioners. They could see what they wanted, take spontaneous side trips, and camp in one place for as long as they liked.

Such mobility made park administration an even bigger headache. Not only did Yellowstone's soldiers serve as ranger-naturalists and game wardens, they now became traffic cops. None of this fit the Army's traditional role. By 1916, 14 other national parks had been established, and it became clear that coordinated administration would benefit them all. Fine-tuning the Army's management model, Congress established the National Park Service to "conserve the scenery and the natural and historic objects and the wild life therein and to provide for the enjoyment of the same in such manner and by

Students, teachers, and a few dads crowd a Park Service fire truck in front of the school at Mammoth Hot Springs. When this photo was snapped in the early 1950s, the building served grades one through six and housed a lending library for Park Service employees. Today the former school, located behind Officer's Row, continues to serve as Mammoth's local library and is a community center and canteen, as well. VERDE WATSON PHOTO

such means as will leave them unimpaired for the enjoyment of future generations."

Today you will see ranger-naturalists in green and gray uniforms in any national park you visit. Just like the soldiers of yesterday, park rangers are trained to answer your questions and enforce regulations. Now, though, they work in tandem with a well-tuned cadre of scientists, historians, education specialists, and planners as the National Park Service fulfills its statutory obligations.

The national park idea that began in Yellowstone more than 125 years ago has led to the establishment of nearly 400 sites throughout the United States where the nation preserves its natural and cultural heritage.

Yellowstone Is Part of an Ecosystem

Whatever the season, and wherever you go in the park, remember that everything you see is connected to everything else. A molten mass of rock close to the earth's surface is the energy source for all of Yellowstone's thermal features. These thermal features, in turn, affect the kinds of plants and animals that can live around them. Only certain plants can grow in or near the heavily mineralized hot springs deposits, and only certain animals can eat those plants. The animals that eat the hot springs plants may be prey to other animals, which may be prey to other animals . . . and so it goes in the food chain of the ecosystem we call Yellowstone.

The mountain building, flooding, volcanic activity, and glaciers that made Yellowstone what it is did not stop at the borders of Yellowstone National Park. Neither do the modern-day impacts of logging, mining, oil and gas drilling, and recreational development.

When the park was established in 1872, the West was still very much a frontier. Aside from the unique geological features that park founders sought to protect, the 2.2 million acres (900,000 ha) of high plateaus, mountain ranges, and crystal waterways blended seamlessly with the surrounding area. Little did the founders know of the far-reaching ramifications future development would have on the unique thermal features, canyon, and lakes they so cherished. Neither did they dream of the complexity of today's decision-making process.

More than 125 years since its founding, Yellowstone National Park is recognized as the heart of a nearly 18-million-acre (7.2 million ha) ecosystem. The Greater Yellowstone Ecosystem also includes Grand Teton National Park, two national wildlife refuges, six national forests, and 13 counties within portions of three states (Wyoming, Montana, and Idaho). Each of these— the park, the refuges, the forests, the counties, and the states—writes its own rules and has its own plan for managing resources, but many are beginning to work cooperatively and creatively.

In 1995, after six years of intense hearings, lobbying, and negotiation, President Bill Clinton proposed a $65 million federal buyout to stop the New World Mine, a gold, copper, and silver mining complex planned just 2.5 miles (4 km) from the park's northeast boundary. The stakes were high.

The mining company planned to build its mine and toxic tailings impoundment at an altitude of 8,000 to 10,000 feet (2,400–3,000 m) in an area of regular earthquake activity. Quake-related floods or landslides could have sent a toxic soup of acid wastes and heavy metals far downstream into the headwaters of three major drainages: Miller Creek, a tributary of Soda Butte Creek, which flows into the park; the Stillwater River, which flows through the Absaroka Wilderness Area; and watersheds that feed the

Yellowstone River, including Soda Butte Creek and another stream that drains into the Clarks Fork of the Yellowstone, Wyoming's only designated Wild and Scenic River. The mine would also have created an unstable boom and bust economy in the tiny gateway community of Cooke City, Montana, and would have encroached on prime grizzly bear habitat.

In 1997, the U.S. Departments of Agriculture and the Interior withdrew more than 22,000 acres (8,800 ha) near the New World Mine site from mining eligibility for 20 years, further protecting the priceless watersheds and wildlife habitat of the Greater Yellowstone Ecosystem.

Recreational development, logging, and oil and gas drilling all around the boundaries of the park threaten grizzly bears, elk, and bison that move seasonally to locations outside the park. The increased noise and bustle from each of these activities force the animals to look for new places to live. Their options are becoming more and more limited.

Livestock producers voice concerns about bison and wolves that drift beyond park boundaries. Their concern often has deadly results for wildlife. The purchase of winter range by the Rocky Mountain Elk Foundation and the U.S. Forest Service has partly met the need for habitat outside the park for other animals, such as elk. Long-term, persistent efforts by the public and the federal government have saved bison, trumpeter swans, and grizzly bears from extinction and have restored the gray wolf to Yellowstone.

The hot springs of Yellowstone harbor an incredible array of life forms in a barely tapped frontier. The study of these life forms holds promise for future problem-solving. Plans to tap thermal features on private land outside Yellowstone's boundaries threaten the park's many hot springs and geysers. All the thermal features within and outside the park are fueled by the same heat source, so tapping one would most certainly affect the others.

The ability to see and understand the interrelationships within an ecosystem is a wonderful gift. So use your eyes, ears, and noses, tread lightly, and enjoy Yellowstone National Park.

The Forests and the Trees

Look closely at the "big three" conifers or evergreens that seem to be everywhere in Yellowstone. At first glance, Engelmann spruce, Douglas-fir, and lodgepole pine may all look alike, but some important features are different. You will soon get the point.

The Engelmann spruce has sharp, stiff, square (if you look at one from its end) needles attached singly to a branch that is covered with needles. This tree prefers shade and is shaped like a pyramid. Its drooping cones are smooth, slightly flexible, and small—2.5 inches (6.4 cm) or smaller. Engelmann spruce trees can live for 350 to 500 years.

The Fires of 1988

In 1988, an unusually wet spring in Yellowstone was followed by the driest summer on record. More than 50 fires—some wild, some caused by people— buttressed by drought and high winds, inspired one of the nation's most expensive and complex firefighting efforts. The fires burned nearly 800,000 acres (320,000 ha) or one-third of the park's lands. The park spent more than $120 million and deployed more than 25,000 firefighters to fight the fires of the Greater Yellowstone Ecosystem.

The human race learned a great lesson that summer: no matter how hard we try, we cannot always control the raw, unbridled power of fire. Even if we employ fire suppression methods as soon as we detect fire, we cannot be sure of containing it.

One of Yellowstone's most widespread fires began with a spark from a woodcutter's cigarette outside park boundaries. Vigorously fought from the very start, the North Fork Fire eventually burned thousands and thousands of acres. It threatened commercial developments and Park Service buildings at Old Faithful, Madison Junction, Norris Geyser Basin, Canyon Village, Tower-Roosevelt Junction, Mammoth Hot Springs, and the gateway community of West Yellowstone, Montana.

At the start of the siege, Park Service policy was to quickly squelch fires caused by people. Natural fires were allowed to burn if they did not threaten human life, property, historic and cultural sites, special natural features, or threatened or endangered species. (This policy remains in effect today. In addition, hazardous fuel loads around the park's structures, developed areas, and backcountry cabins are reduced by prescribed burning and mechanical removal— to better allow naturally ignited fires to burn their natural course.)

But by midsummer in 1988, the natural fires covered by the "let-it-burn" policy were growing quickly. Extreme weather conditions and accumulations of heavy, dry fuel fanned the flames. On July 21, 1988, 17,000 acres (6,800 ha) were burning. The Park Service suspended official policy and focused efforts on extinguishing all of the fires.

At the operation's peak, 9,000 firefighters, more than 100 fire engines, and dozens of helicopters from many states were on the scene. But more often than not, normal firefighting techniques proved useless. September snows finally quelled the fires of 1988.

The Yellowstone fires defied the logic and on-the-ground research of the ablest professional firefighters. Over the course of the summer, the fires moved fast, often at a rate of 5 to 10 miles (8–16 km) a day. "Spotting"—when wind-carried embers sparked blazes up to 1.5 miles (2.4 km) ahead of the main fires—enabled the fires to cross the Grand Canyon of the Yellowstone River, as well as other rivers and roads that would normally have served as barriers. These spot fires created the fire mosaic that we see today—burned areas interspersed with unburned areas.

The Douglas-fir has flat, flexible, and friendly (no sharp points) needles spiraling around twiggy branches. Not a true fir, the Douglas-fir is related to the hemlock and is shaped somewhat like the Engelmann spruce.

Three-pronged bracts poke out between the scales of its hanging cones. The thick bark of the Douglas-fir helps make it fire resistant. Like the Englemann spruce, the Douglas-fir is a long-lived tree.

Most of the lodgepole pines you see grow in "toothpick forests," so tightly packed together that their lower branches die and fall off for lack of sunlight. Because lodgepole pines are "self-pruning" and have straight, even trunks, Native Americans used them as poles for their tepees and lodges; hence the name. When a lodgepole pine grows all by itself, its shape is more or less like that of the spruce or fir, with full branches all the way to the ground. A tree like this can live more than 300 years.

Lodgepole pine needles are attached in pairs. The tree produces two types of cones to ensure that the species survives. One is like other conifer cones: it opens

Engelmann Spruce

Douglas-Fir

Lodgepole Pine

at maturity and its seeds are carried by wind or animals and scattered on the forest floor. Since the lodgepole pine is shade-intolerant, you seldom see young lodgepoles in "toothpick forests" where these seeds germinate.

The second type of lodgepole pine cone is serotinous, or sealed for delayed seed dispersal. Fire quickly kills the thin-barked trees, but within a couple of days these serotinous cones pop open, spreading seeds that grow readily in the nutrient-rich earth of the scorched forest floor. Lodgepole pines are called "pioneers" because they are among the first plants to grow after a fire or other habitat disturbance.

Pioneering is the first stage of "succession," a continuous process through which a series of plant communities gradually evolves to a "climax" community. A climax community is stable and capable of perpetuating itself. Subalpine fir is the climax species in 60 percent of Yellowstone's forested habitat, but, because of poor soils and the fir's need for shade and moisture, you will seldom find a stand made up solely of subalpine fir.

The type of vegetation you will see in different parts of the park depends on annual precipitation (which comes mostly in the form of snow), elevation, and bedrock. Together, these elements have created zones where one vegetative type predominates, but others aren't excluded. Yellowstone's vegetative zones include the spruce-fir, the lodgepole pine, and the Douglas-fir zones (all within the subalpine fir habitat), plus the alpine and the Great Basin zones. Young stands in any of the subalpine fir zones may be dominated by pioneer lodgepole pines, with other species sprouting here and there on the forest floor. In mature stands, the overstory, or the uppermost layer of vegetation, may be dominated by climax species.

The spruce-fir zone is found at higher elevations, along the margins of ponds, in drainages, and on north-facing slopes where precipitation is greater than 40 inches (101.6 cm) a year. These trees thrive in ancient volcanic soils at elevations above 8,400 feet (2,520 m). Young stands in the spruce-fir zone may be dominated by lodgepole pines, with spruce and fir in the understory.

The lodgepole pine zone spreads throughout the central portion of the park, at middle elevations of 7,600 to 8,400 feet (2,280–2,520 m). Precipitation levels are relatively low here and volcanic soils are poor in nutrients. This zone comprises about half of the park.

The Douglas-fir zone can be identified by its grasslands. At the lower altitudes—6,000 to 7,600 feet (1,800–2,280 m)—along the Yellowstone and Lamar river valleys, this zone features sometimes scattered, sometimes dense stands of Douglas-fir and aspen. The tree clusters dot open areas of grass and sagebrush that grow in sediments from long-ago glaciers. Less than 20 inches (50.8 cm) of precipitation fall here each year.

The alpine zone is the highest, occurring in areas above 10,000 feet (3,000 m) throughout the park. Many of the wildflowers, shrubs, and trees found at lower elevations are present here, but in alpine form, growing low and compact to survive the shortened growing season and harsh conditions.

The Great Basin zone is in a small area along the northern boundary of the park. Here, low elevation, little moisture—less than 15 inches (38.1 cm) of annual precipitation—and heavy shale soils create ideal habitat for grasses and woody shrubs.

In each of these vegetative zones, the exception—the presence of other plant types—is the rule.

Wind, flood, fire, insect infestation, and other subtle and not-so-subtle catastrophes affect all of these zones. The 1988 fires, a natural event that hit Yellowstone hard, allowed lodgepole pines to germinate and thrive. They continue to be the most common tree in the park.

In most places, the fires killed the trees but only burned the tops off of other plants. Where water was present or available, regrowth began within days of the fires' passing. In drier soils, the waiting seeds, rhizomes, bulbs, and root crowns stayed dormant until the following spring, when soil moisture was replenished by winter snows. In most places, the fires burned less than an inch into the soil and enriched it with nutrients. With sunlight and precipitation, the seeds and nutrients produced a mat of shrubs, flowers, grasses, and tree seedlings the following spring. Where fires had burned for several hours, the soil was burned to a greater depth. These areas took longer to recover.

Eighty percent of Yellowstone is covered by forest habitat, but since the fires of 1988, the forested areas are not characterized by a solid green screen. Throughout Yellowstone you will see blackened trees, some on the ground and others still upright.

The dead standing trees were killed when fire moved quickly through a stand, sometimes in a matter of seconds. The fire consumed all needles and twigs and drove out the trees' moisture, but not to the point that the trees ignited. The next winter, elk stripped the bark from the trunks to reach the sweet cambium underneath. For 40 to 60 years, these fire-killed trees may remain vertical, providing valuable habitat for three-toed and hairy woodpeckers, northern flickers, and mountain bluebirds.

In many places around Yellowstone, you need only lower your eyes to see the new living trees. Forest succession has begun. Where mature Engelmann spruce and Douglas-fir trees once grew, you will see pioneering lodgepole pines, all of a similar size.

Fire and Ice

Just about anywhere you go in Yellowstone, you are riding, walking, sitting, or standing right over a "hot spot" of magma. Depending on where you are, the magma may be anywhere from 2 to 6 miles (3.2–9.6 km) beneath the surface. Most of the North American continental crust is 20 miles (32 km) above molten material. Yellowstone's hot springs and geysers are steamy proof that the magma deep down is still "cooking."

Adults may remember when Mount St. Helens blew its top in 1980. Ash from this volcano in southwestern Washington spread all across the western states. Yellowstone's first and biggest blast, 2.1 million years ago, exploded with *2,400 times* the force of Mount St. Helens and spread its sulfuric ash from California to Iowa. That volcanic eruption, which was far bigger than any volcanic eruption in recorded history, and two other more recent ones, helped form the dynamic landscape we know today as Yellowstone National Park.

How a Mountain Forms

Two billion seven hundred million years ago, pressures deep beneath the earth's crust pushed on that surface, breaking and folding it over on itself and turning some of it on edge. To see how this process works, lay your hands beside each other, palms down, on mud or wet sand. Slowly press your hands together until they make a kind of tent on the flat surface. Watch how the mud or sand moves and breaks away as it rises between your hands. Then slowly remove your hands, and you will see that the material you squished to form your tent is wrinkled and folded.

Notice how cracks or fractures resulted from your mountain building, just like they did on a grand scale as some of the mountains formed in Yellowstone. Magma, a mixture of hot melted rock and gas deep inside the earth, sometimes oozed like toothpaste through those fractures (or faults, geologically speaking). At other times, pressure deep inside the earth rushed the magma to the surface in volcanic eruptions.

Once it surfaced, either by oozing or explosion, the magma, now called lava, cooled and hardened. More magma was pushed to the surface and spilled over, covering the first layer of lava. This second layer also cooled and hardened. Sometimes the process repeated itself until the layers formed a new mountain.

But volcanoes are just one part of the park's geologic history. Earthquakes, seas, and glaciers are also part of the story. Learning a little about these ancient forces—and about how they still affect the region—will help you better understand all that you see and experience in Yellowstone.

The Beartooth Mountain Range on the park's eastern border and the Snake River Plain to the south were formed during an intense period of mountain building and volcanic eruptions 2.7 *billion* years ago—long before there were people, trees, or even dinosaurs.

It is hard to imagine how long ago that was, so let's look at it this way: If you could step back in time, and one step equalled 100 years, your first step would take you to the late nineteenth century, when visitors toured the park by stagecoach. Now, to reach the period when the park's geologic features began forming, you would have to walk across the United States five times or about halfway around the world—a total distance of about 15,000 miles (24,000 km)!

The Inland Seas

After the first period of mountain building, seas flooded the Yellowstone region from time to time. The water stretched from Canada to Mexico, covering all but the highest peaks. Then the sea receded, and another flood came and went. This cycle continued for many, many years.

Each time the seas flooded Yellowstone, sand, silt, clay, limy mud, and other sediments settled to the bottom. As the water evaporated, these sediments solidified. On the slopes of Mount Everts, near the northern boundary of the park, you can see evidence of the many times Yellowstone was a seabed. Look for the "layer cake" effect of sandstones, shales, and limestone. Elsewhere in Yellowstone, ancient seabeds are less recognizable because their layers were severely twisted and broken by later mountain-building episodes.

Thermal Mountain Building

Fifty million years ago, the last great sea disappeared and a new mountain-building period began. Magma once again found its way to the surface and erupted in a series of volcanoes that created the Absaroka Mountains. Both the Absaroka and the Washburn mountain ranges show the rubbly vestiges of Yellowstone's first significant period of volcanism. Ash and lava overtook whole forests. You can see evidence of those forests in the petrified remnants on Specimen Ridge.

Look Inside the Earth's Interior

Whenever you visit the geothermal features that make Yellowstone famous, you will see geology happening right before your eyes.

We use both "geothermal" and "hydrothermal" to describe Yellowstone's hot-water features. "Geo" means earth, "hydro" means water, and "thermal" means heat. So "geothermal" refers to heat from the earth's interior and "hydrothermal" refers to water heated by a magmatic source.

Ten thousand geothermal features are scattered throughout the park. Most of these features are clustered in a few areas called geyser basins. The geysers and hot springs are here because magma from the most recent volcanoes is still very hot about 2 miles (3.2 km) beneath the earth's surface. Underground temperatures have remained about the same since the park began to keep records more than 100 years ago.

Abundant water feeds the hot springs—each winter as much as 200 inches (508 cm) of snow falls on the park, settling into a 5-foot-thick (1.5 m) blanket. When summer comes, the snow melts and water flows into the rivers and lakes and seeps into the huge natural underground reservoirs. Hot rocks deep in the earth heat the water. The heated water expands in the enclosed space, causing pressure to build, and the pressure forces the water (as superheated water and steam) back to the surface, creating hot springs, fumaroles, and geysers.

Then, 2.1 million years ago, a magma dome pushed up the earth's crust and grew. Cracks developed around the perimeter of the growing dome, eventually reaching the magma chamber below. The pressurized magma that the dome had held in check burst through the cracks, spewing lava and ash over the region. Without adequate support, the dome collapsed, creating the Huckleberry Ridge Caldera, which extended more than 45 miles (75 km) from Island Park in Idaho to the central part of Yellowstone. Lava continued to ooze through fissures in the caldera, or crater, floor (the roof of the collapsed magma dome), adding layer upon layer of volcanic debris to the landscape and creating a plateau that extended throughout much of Yellowstone.

Another smaller caldera at Island Park was formed 1.3 million years ago. Then, about 600,000 years ago, or, if you step back in time, less than 0.5 mile (0.8 km), a new magma dome developed. Fissures around this dome eventually provided the molten material with direct pipelines to the surface, setting the scene for violent explosions greater than any in recorded history. A series of rapid, cataclysmic eruptions quickly spread hundreds of cubic miles of hot rocks and ash over the central portion of Yellowstone, once again filling canyons and valleys where water had worn away the volcanic debris of earlier eruptions.

Thus the still-smoldering Lava Creek or Yellowstone Caldera was formed and, at the same time, partially filled to a depth of 1,000 feet (300 m). It became the low and rolling Central Plateau that encompasses one-third of the park's area. Second in size only to the Huckleberry Ridge Caldera, the Yellowstone Caldera is 28 miles (44.8 km) across, 47 miles (75.2 km) wide, and about 1 mile (1.6 km) deep.

A smaller caldera inside the giant Yellowstone Caldera formed 150,000 years ago in the area of West Thumb. Finally, 70,000 years ago, a last lava

Make Your Own Geyser

● ● ● ● ● ● ● ● ● ● ● ● ● ● ● ● ● ●

Put a glass funnel upside down in the bottom of a shallow pan nearly filled with water. Place a nail under one side of the funnel to allow water to enter your "underground reservoir." Now heat the pan of water on the stove. As the hot water releases steam, air bubbles will force water up through the neck of the funnel. Your geyser erupts because the bubbles in the heated water create an underwater pressure greater than the downward pressure of the air in the funnel.

flow formed the Pitchstone Plateau southwest of Yellowstone Lake.

Two resurgent domes on the floor of the Yellowstone Caldera continue to rise and fall. Measurements since 1923 show Mallard Lake Dome, just east of Old Faithful, and Sour Creek Dome, north of Yellowstone Lake, have bulged and subsided an average of 1 inch (2.5 cm) each year.

Faults in the Yellowstone and West Thumb calderas allow water to seep down into the permeable volcanic rock, where it is heated by the magma below. That superheated water returns to the surface to be released as hot water and steam by geysers, hot springs, mud pots, and fumaroles.

Yellowstone's 10,000 geothermal features fall into these four categories. They are four different outcomes of the same process—groundwater, heated by underground magma, returning to the earth's surface.

When heated water rises to the surface of the ground through a series of tubes (similar to the pipes that deliver water to your faucets), it forms *hot springs*. Sometimes the water collects in pools, and sometimes the pools spill over, creating terraces like those at Mammoth Hot Springs.

Steam vents or *fumaroles* are hot springs with limited water supplies. Their underground channels pipe very little groundwater to the hot rocks below, where the water instantly converts to steam and quickly exits with a hiss or a roar.

When surface water collects around fumaroles, it mixes with sulfur-laden steam to produce sulfuric acid. The acid dissolves the surrounding clay and mud and forms bubbly *mud pots*. This chain reaction releases hydrogen sulfide, that familiar rotten-egg or firecracker smell associated with hot springs. Mud pots are most active from winter through early summer, when snow and rain help moisten the mud.

Geysers are hot springs with more complicated plumbing systems. In fact, no two geysers have the same size, shape, and arrangement of tubes and chambers through which water passes on its way to and from the surface.

While we cannot see the actual plumbing of a geyser, scientists can guess how it works. As with hot springs, superheated water and gas rise in

Thermophiles

The next time you are watching a crime show on television and the case is cracked because of DNA fingerprinting, think of Yellowstone.

In 1967, in a Yellowstone hot spring of more than 176 degrees F (80°C), Thomas Brock discovered a cigar-shaped microorganism that was one of earth's very first life forms, one that holds the key to deciphering the code of life. Brock's *Thermus aquaticus (Taq)* is a thermophile, an organism that thrives in a warm environment.

About 25 years after Brock's discovery, Kary Mullis used an enzyme from *Taq* in a special process he developed to copy and amplify the DNA within living cells. DNA contains the genes that make up a blueprint of life, determining in humans, for example, physical characteristics such as height, eye shade, and hair color. For his achievement, Mullis received the Nobel prize for chemistry in 1993.

Using the *Taq* enzyme, scientists can now identify a crime suspect from one blood cell. The enzyme may someday be used to detect AIDS, genetic diseases, and genes which cause birth defects.

Scientists are using other heat-stable thermophiles from Yellowstone's hot springs to produce alternative fuels, food additives, environmentally friendly road deicers, and antibiotics; still others are useful in ore, paper, and pulp processing and paint removal. Thermophiles have spawned a multibillion-dollar industry.

Even NASA is interested in Yellowstone's thermophiles. Filaments of ancient living organisms are suspended in a nonliving state in the most hostile environments imaginable, much like those found on Mars. What scientists call the "biogeochemical signature" of these organisms can be detected in satellite imagery and compared to images of active volcanoes and suspected hot springs data on the red planet as NASA searches for evidence of extraterrestrial life.

In Yellowstone, public and private collection of biological specimens for research dates back to the nineteenth century, a precedent that has allowed lucrative private use of public natural resources. Recognizing that the study and cloning of heat-stable microorganisms for commercial development has far-reaching significance, in 1997, the Park Service, for the first time, entered into an agreement that ensures the park and its programs will share in specific economic and scientific benefits resulting from commercial bioprospecting and research of microbes sampled from the park's geothermal features.

According to Yellowstone's chief of research, John Varley, the historic benefit-sharing agreement with Diversa Corporation of San Diego, California, is a thoughtful and rational approach to research conducted on park resources: "It's good for science, good for parks, and good for the citizens of our country."

Allowing research, commercial or otherwise, on Yellowstone's thermal features may seem like opening Pandora's box. But instead of releasing evils and miseries, the contents of the thermal pools may provide keys to solving some of the greatest problems of humankind. John Varley says the park's hot springs harbor more biodiversity than the Brazilian rainforests, and 99 percent of the species that live in Yellowstone's hot waters are yet to be identified.

underground tubes, but somewhere along the line they get stuck for a time, causing pressure to build enormously. The pressure becomes so great that the "dam" bursts. Water and gas surge to the ground's surface, quickly decreasing the pressure and causing the geyser to erupt. When the geyser's tubes and chambers are nearly empty, the eruption ends. The underground reservoir begins refilling with groundwater, and the cycle repeats.

Each geyser has a unique cycle. Some spout nearly all the time, while others have quiet intervals that last days, months, and even years.

The word "geyser" comes from the Icelandic word "geysir," which means to gush or rage. Major geysers can also be found in New Zealand, Chile, and the Kamchatka Peninsula in the northwest corner of the Russian Federation.

Nearly all geysers and many hot springs build mounds or terraces made up of minerals. The hot water deposits minerals in very thin layers that pile up over hundreds of years. Each layer is a crust or film of rock-forming mineral that was once dissolved in hot water. This mineral-laden water surfaced through complex geothermal plumbing. Then, the minerals settled out because they were heavier than their watery carrier. To understand this process, think about how salt quickly dissolves when you add it to hot water. If you leave a puddle of this salty water on the counter and allow the water to evaporate, the salt reappears as a thin film.

Like a film of salt, hot springs deposits are fundamentally white or gray. Yet many of the thermal features found in Yellowstone appear brightly colored

Grandparents can share their wonder of Yellowstone's awesome natural resources.
Mike Snyder photo

because the rock, constantly underwater or flushed with water, provides ideal habitat for heat-loving cyanobacteria or algae. Which one of these lives in a particular thermal environment depends on the water's acidity or alkalinity and the rock sediment's mineral content. Dissolved minerals piped upward through thermal plumbing also may tint the new rocks or pools.

Cyanobacteria and many other types of primitive microorganisms appear in and around Yellowstone's thermal areas. They are descendants of similar microorganisms that once nearly blanketed the earth, creating an oxygenated atmosphere that would eventually support life. Cyanobacteria were among the first organisms known to carry out photosynthesis, the process by which carbon dioxide and water use light as an energy source to produce simple sugars and oxygen.

First appearing yellow and orange, then green, red, and brown, cyanobacteria thrive in neutral or alkaline water that has cooled to at least 163 degrees F (73°C). Cyanobacteria live in the Lower, Midway, Upper, and West Thumb geyser basins, and at Mammoth Hot Springs. Norris Geyser Basin also has some cyanobacteria, despite its acidity.

Cyanobacteria are "thermophilic": they are able to live at high temperatures. Some thermophiles have been discovered in Yellowstone's hot springs that have far-reaching ramifications for modern life.

Color in the thermal basins is also derived from mineral content and algal thermophiles that grow on the hot springs deposits. Brightly colored minerals, such as silica, iron, and sulfur, coat the walls and bottoms of hot springs or remain suspended in the water. Primitive plants called algae may be green, yellow, or brown and may make a hot spring pool or deposit appear that color. The heat and acidity of the water determine what type of algae is present. Extremely hot springs, whether neutral, alkaline, or acidic, are colorless, but they appear deep blue because they reflect the color of the sky overhead.

Many of the trees around Yellowstone's hot springs wear peculiar white "tube socks," evidence that they are being petrified right before your eyes. These were living trees, but when hot springs formed or spread around them, the water gradually choked them with heat and replaced woody fiber with dissolved minerals. What you see are vertical fossils in the making.

Earthquakes

Another kind of geologic change occurs daily in Yellowstone, although chances are you will be unaware of it. Each day, an average of five earth tremors shake the park and the surrounding area. This is normal activity for a region with such a violent history of previous earthquakes and volcanism. Most of the tremors are so slight that you will not feel them, but you can see them recorded on the seismograph at the Old Faithful Visitor Center. Seismographs are sensitive instruments that detect and record the intensity, direction, and duration of earth movements. The Old Faithful seismograph sometimes records as many as 100 earthquakes a day.

Once in a human lifetime, a big one shakes the park. On August 17, 1959, the biggest earthquake in Yellowstone's recorded history hit the Madison Valley, along the park's western boundary. The Hebgen Lake earthquake was centered about 12 miles (19.2 km) north of West Yellowstone. Much of the earth in a 200-square-mile (320 km²) area, including Hebgen Lake, sank between 1 and 20 feet (0.3–6 m). A huge landslide trapped 250 campers, killing 28 of them, and dammed the Madison River, forming Earthquake Lake.

Soon after the quake hit, nearly 300 geysers and hot springs erupted inside the park. Some long-dormant geysers erupted immediately, and 160 others erupted for the first time. Some geysers erupted with much greater force or frequency than usual, and others stopped erupting entirely and have not spouted since. The Hebgen Lake earthquake caused noticeable water level changes in wells as far away as Puerto Rico to the east and Hawaii to the west.

If you leave or enter the park through Yellowstone's West Entrance in the summer, stop at the USDA Forest Service visitor center at the top of the slide that formed Earthquake Lake.

Yellowstone will always be an unsettled place. Its long history of volcanic activity and earth movements means that someday—probably not in your lifetime—things will fly sky-high once again. As you explore the park, you will constantly be reminded of how quickly what you see today can change. The hot water and steam that come from deep in the earth will build up and tear down formations as you watch.

Change is inevitable, especially in Yellowstone. Scientists say any new volcanic activity in the Yellowstone region will probably be preceded by increased gas emissions and localized earthquakes as strong or stronger than the Hebgen Lake earthquake. But don't worry; the park's network of seismic monitoring stations should give you plenty of warning if something big is about to happen.

Rivers of Ice

You may notice the effects of another kind of specialized geological event as you tour the park—glaciation. During the quiet times between the later volcanic eruptions, all but the highest mountain peaks and the western edge of the park were again flooded—this time by ice. Three major periods of glaciation, between 200,000 and 15,000 years ago, recarved the landscape. The last glaciers covered about 90 percent of the park.

Glaciers are moving rivers of ice, formed when the winter's snowpack is so deep all of it cannot possibly melt in the summer. High in the mountains, the weight of each winter's accumulation of new snow crushes the oldest snow on the bottom, turning it to ice. Each winter, the snow-covered icefield thickens; each summer, some of the snow on top melts. The water seeps into the bottom layer where it is frozen by the snow-turned-ice. The process repeats itself year after year until at last the whole icefield gets so heavy it begins to slide downhill. The ice is now a glacier.

Unlike a liquid river, a glacier moves extremely slowly, scouring the sides of mountains and tearing off huge chunks of rock. The frozen river picks up giant boulders, smaller rocks, sand, and clay. All are suspended in the ice until the glacier reaches lower and warmer elevations. There, it finally begins to melt, move faster, and deposit its debris. You will see lonesome boulders called glacial erratics scattered throughout Yellowstone. The melting glaciers dropped them off as they lightened their loads. Notice how the edges of these boulders are round and smooth, like pebbles in a stream. Sand and other debris wore away any sharp points on these rocks as they moved within the glaciers.

The scraping, grinding glaciers also gouged out bowl-shaped depressions called cirques high in the mountains. You can see cirques in the Absaroka Range and elsewhere around the park. Some of the glacial debris clogged valleys, blocking natural streamflows and creating lakes and ponds. Once in a while, these glacial dams burst and caused floods, pushing more rocks and debris along in front of them.

A few snowfields remain in Yellowstone's high mountains year-round, but the park's last glaciers melted about 10,000 years ago.

A National Park Is Not a Zoo

You won't see any iron bars or fences during your visit to Yellowstone National Park. You won't see trained animals doing tricks. What you will see, if you are lucky, are wild bison, moose, elk, deer, pronghorn antelope, wolves, and countless birds and other animals in their natural environment. Some migrate outside the park seasonally, but they always come back. Instinct tells them this is their home.

Some of the animals wear collars with radio transmitters; these allow researchers to gather data on the animals and their habits from a distance. Such information helps scientists better understand habitat needs. It also helps the park fulfill its stewardship role.

How many animals you see during your visit to Yellowstone will depend on many factors, including the time of year, the time of day, the weather,

Don't Feed the Bears

If your parents or grandparents visited Yellowstone in the 1960s or earlier, they may have told you that bears were everywhere. Bold black bears would stop cars along the highway to beg for food, creating "bear jams" that backed up traffic. The bears milled from vehicle to vehicle, looking for handouts, sometimes damaging cars and injuring tourists.

From the park's early days onward, black bears and grizzlies gathered nightly at hotel garbage pits, as well as in the open dumps of Yellowstone's gateway communities. Concessioners even built a fenced enclosure with bleachers inside just south of the Grand Canyon of the Yellowstone River. Each night, hundreds of visitors could safely watch 50 to 60 bears tussle and gorge on garbage scattered about on a raised concrete platform. Park rangers would capture this "teachable moment" by lecturing on the bears' natural history.

Since Yellowstone's "exceedingly tame" bears were a "never-failing source of delight to the tourist," as one guidebook noted, and human food was readily accessible to the bears, conflicts between humans and bears were inevitable. Between 1931 and 1969, an average of 46 people were injured *each year*. Black bears, the least aggressive of Yellowstone's resident bears, were involved in almost all of these incidents.

In the late 1960s and early 1970s, the National Park Service closed the garbage dumps and enforced a "no feeding" rule along the highways. Conflicts increased for a few years, but then diminished as the bears returned to natural food sources. The success of the park's new policy shows that bears living in a wild state are far less dangerous than bears that have become habituated to humans and human food.

and human disturbance. In the summer, animals tend to be less active during the heat of the day, so look for them in the very early morning or in the late evening. In the winter, many animals are easier to see because they must spend their days in the open, constantly foraging for food. All animals will seek shelter if it is rainy or stormy, just like you do.

One of the most important keys to animal watching is knowing something about animal habits. Use binoculars, a camera telephoto lens, or a spotting scope to scan habitat edges where forest and meadow meet. Watch for circling ravens, eagles, or hawks; they may show you where a wolf or a bear is eating its prey. Be still and listen. Instead of worrying about perfect photographs, consider buying the excellent images offered for sale by park concessioners, and use your time in Yellowstone to truly observe and to learn more about what you see.

Wherever you go in the park, remember, DON'T FEED THE ANIMALS. And make sure you give them lots of room. Though many animals look tame, all wildlife is wild and potentially dangerous. When you are hiking, make lots of noise to avoid startling animals that may then become defensive. Never hike alone. Never try to get close to animals. Remember, this is their home. You are a visitor.

Bears: Black bears, the smallest and most widely distributed bears in North America, are only about 3 feet (0.9 m) high at the shoulder. Boars (males) average 210 to 315 pounds (95–143 kg) and sows (females) weigh 135 to 160 pounds (61–73 kg). Black bears have fair eyesight and an exceptional sense of smell. In the wild, they eat an omnivorous diet of grass, berries, tree bark, insects, fish, carrion, and newborn ungulates—hooved mammals like deer, elk, and pronghorns. Using their short, curved claws, black bears can easily climb trees to feed on bird eggs, fruit, and seeds, or to beat a quick retreat if they feel threatened.

Grizzly bears share the black bears' diet and extend it to include roots, which they can easily dig with their longer curved claws. These animal tools are as long as the fingers of adult men. Grizzlies also have dished faces and tubular snouts that pick up the faintest of smells. While black bears range in color from black to blond, grizzlies are light brown to black with silver-tipped or grizzled hairs that seem to ripple on their prominent humps as they walk. This unique coloration gave rise to the nickname "silvertip."

Grizzlies are massive and more aggressive than black bears. On all fours, the adults measure 3.5 to 4.5 feet (1–1.4 m) from the ground to their humps,

Ranging from black to blond, the black bear is commonly mistaken for the grizzly bear.
MIKE SAMPLE PHOTO

The majestic grizzly bear has a humped neck and dished face. MIKE SAMPLE PHOTO

but when they stand on their hind legs for a better whiff or view, they may be more than 8 feet (2.4 m) tall. Boars typically weigh 400 to 600 pounds (200–300 kg) and sows weigh 250 to 350 pounds (125–175 kg). Grizzlies can climb trees, especially when they are young, and they can sprint up- and downhill and on the flat at speeds of up to 45 miles per hour (75 kph).

In winter, both black bears and grizzlies hibernate in caves or dens. Since the bears' vital signs—body temperature, respiration, and circulation—do not decrease as significantly as they do in other hibernating animals, bears are easily awakened and, in fact, sometimes leave their dens for short periods during the winter.

In mid- to late January, or even February for grizzlies, pregnant sows barely rouse themselves and give birth, usually to two or three cubs. Cubs are born blind, furless, and toothless and spend the rest of the winter nursing and sleeping. Black bear cubs stay with their mothers through only one more winter, after which the sow drives them away so she can breed again. Grizzly sows chase off their cubs after two full winters, so they can mate and bear young every third year. Both black bears and grizzlies live 15 to 20 years in the wild.

Except during mating season, which is late June to early July for black bears and mid-May to late July for grizzlies, bears are solitary animals. A boar black bear's home range may be anywhere from 6 to 124 square miles (9.6–198.4 km²); a sow requires one-third the space. Each male grizzly needs 813 square miles (2,106 km²) of territory. A grizzly sow needs only about one-fourth of that, but still, she needs more than a boar black bear.

The grizzly's awesome need for solitude and habitat (food, water, and shelter) makes its presence a prime indicator of the quality of a wilderness. Yellowstone is one of the few remaining places in the lower 48 states where the threatened grizzly bear has room to roam. In 1996, the Greater Yellowstone Ecosystem had around 350 resident grizzlies and 550 resident black bears.

During the eight months of the year they are awake, bears are walking stomachs, so many areas of the park are closed to visitors to avoid conflicts between humans and bears. Your chances of seeing a bear in Yellowstone may not be as good as they used to be, but several thousand people a year do see bears by using binoculars, camera telephoto lenses, or spotting scopes to scan open, grassy areas like the Hayden Valley and the slopes of Mount Washburn. If you visit the geyser basins in the early spring or late fall, you might just catch a black bear or a grizzly looking for a meal.

Bighorn Sheep: With their dusky tan coats, curved horns, and primeval stares, Yellowstone's 250 Rocky Mountain bighorn sheep seem a lot like time travelers, and indeed they are. Many biologists believe these modern relics are nearly the same as the bighorn sheep that inhabited Yellowstone more than 10,000 years ago when the last glaciers left the high country.

In summer, the bighorns roam the craggy sanctuaries of the Washburn, Gallatin, and Absaroka mountain ranges where they forage on alpine and subalpine grasses, herbs, and woody plants. They sometimes appear on Dunraven Pass and in Gardner Canyon, bringing traffic to a standstill. In the winter, bighorns move to lower elevations, competing for forage with elk and deer along the Yellowstone and Lamar rivers.

Members of the cattle family, bighorns live in herds throughout the year. During the late autumn rut, the rams fight furiously for ewes, crashing headlong into each other with their impressive spiraling horns. After such severe headbanging, the rams may act punch-drunk, but their wooziness is usually short-lived. The rams' horns, which continue growing throughout their lives, are attached to ossicones—calcified masses that dissipate force and protect the rams from brain damage.

Each spiky-horned ewe produces one or two lambs in late spring. Lambs grow quickly and are soon playing tag and follow-the-leader. These games emulate the bighorns' response to danger when one animal, usually a ewe, leads the herd swiftly up a mountain as high as it can go, sometimes right over the top. Concave, spongy feet enable bighorns to leap steadily from one rock to another and move quickly out of harm's way.

Bison: Only in a national park would tourists try to snap a close-up of an animal the same size as the family car. Every year someone tries for that perfect photo of an American bison and is killed, gored, or otherwise injured in the process. Bison are wild and unpredictable, just like every other animal in Yellowstone National Park. To top it off, they are ill-tempered, surprisingly agile, and can accelerate to speeds of more than 30 miles per hour (50 kph). It is best to watch them from a distance.

Another member of the cattle family, the bison is the largest land mammal in North America. Bulls commonly weigh more than 2,000 pounds (1,000 kg); cows weigh half as much. It is often hard to tell them apart since both bulls and cows sport curved horns, thick hair on the front half of the body, and beards. Observe them closely, though, and you will see that the cows' horns are more slender and slightly more curved than bulls', their bodies are less massive, and their beards are less prominent.

Adult bison have no large predators to fear, but small predators can make them miserable. During the summer, tiny insects burrow into the bison's shaggy coats, chomp down, and make their massive hosts itch like crazy. To find relief, the bison rub their backs on trees or large rocks, or they may wallow in dirt or sand, techniques they also use to get rid of itchy winter coats. Often, bison get help from brown-headed cowbirds, or buffalo birds, that perch on their backs and feed on the pesky parasites. In the warmest months, you will see this "buddy system" wherever you find bison.

About 2,000 bison roam Yellowstone in large herds of cows, calves, and some bulls. Most mature bulls remain solitary until breeding season in late July and August when they rejoin the herd and duel over cows. Single calves are born in late April and May. Within a couple of days, calves can follow the herd as it moves from one grassy range to another. Bison typically live 12 to 15 years, although occasionally one lives to be 40 years old.

In the winter, more and more bison are ranging outside the park boundaries. Some scientists theorize that roads plowed and groomed for snowmobiling facilitate the bison's migration, as well as their movements within the park. Without the stress of moving through deep snow, more bison than normal may be surviving the winters, perhaps pushing their population to unnaturally high levels. For more than two decades, bison leaving the park have been shot in an effort to control the introduction of brucellosis, a disease that causes domestic cattle to abort their first-born calves. In late 1996, the capture and slaughter of brucellosis-infected bison was introduced as an additional management tool. You can read more about bison and brucellosis on page 92–93 of the guide's, "Northeast Entrance to Tower-Roosevelt Junction."

Yellowstone National Park is the only place in the lower 48 states where wild bison have lived since prehistoric times. Look for bison year-round on the Northern Range (which includes the Lamar and Yellowstone river valleys from Soda Butte to the North Entrance) and along the Madison and Firehole rivers. In the summer, the Hayden Valley is a good place to see bison. In winter, you may see them in smaller numbers in the Pelican and Hayden valleys.

People often refer to bison as "buffalo," a name that was borrowed from the bison's oxlike European cousin as early as 1635. Both are members of the family Bovidae, but "bison" is the proper name for the North American *Bison bison.*

Deer: The mule deer swivels its large ears to pick up the slightest sound. At the first hint of danger, it bounds away. A keen sense of hearing helps this animal survive. Named for its extra-large ears, the Rocky Mountain mule deer enjoys the widest distribution of any subspecies of large game animal on the continent.

During the summer, about 2,500 mule deer live in areas of broken forests and meadows scattered throughout most of Yellowstone. After the rut (or breeding season) in October and November, they migrate to lower, more protected areas like the Gardner Basin just north of the park. When deep snows leave the high country, the herds return to the park.

Mature does bear twin fawns in mid-June. During the next fall's breeding season, older bucks drive away the male fawns, while the females remain with their mothers. By this time, the young bucks have sprouted spindly spike antlers, which they, like the other males, will drop sometime between mid-January and April. Bucks use their antlers to attract does ("Look at my antlers! I will father the biggest and hardiest offspring!") and to fight other bucks for breeding privileges.

After the rut, the top of a buck's head hardens and his antlers easily fall off or snap off at the base. Bucks are truly soreheads for about ten days; after that, their new antlers begin growing. Antlers are actually fast-growing bones. Initially, a velvety skin covers them, helping to protect and bring blood to the antlers as they grow. Around August, the blood stops flowing to the antlers, the antlers harden, and the buck thrashes its antlers against small trees, scraping off the velvet and preparing to challenge other bucks in the fall rut.

Members of the deer family, like cows, are ruminants, or cud-chewing animals. Their stomachs are divided into four compartments, and they regurgitate partially digested food from the first compartment to chew as cud. Mule deer find all the nutrients they need in grasses, forbs (broad-leafed herbs), shrubs, and trees. In winter, they eat anything they can to survive. They strip the bark off trees and paw the snow with their cloven (split) hooves to reach food below.

Only occasionally do visitors see white-tailed deer in Yellowstone.

Elk: More elk live in Yellowstone than in any other place in the world. Not surprisingly, elk outnumber all of Yellowstone's other grazing animals. Parkwide, the summer population is about 31,000.

In summer, look for elk in high meadows throughout the park, where they graze on grasses. Like their cousins the moose, elk also browse on shrubs, aspen bark, and pine needles. In winter, some of the herds move to lower elevations outside the park. Many of the winter resident herds stay around the Northern Range. Since elk tend to stick to lower elevations and hang out around thermal areas, winter visitors often see them at close range.

The fires of 1988 gave elk a new and unexpected food source to help them through the following winter. By burning the bark of lodgepole pines, the fire transformed something that was usually indigestible to elk into a food as good as most winter browse. One advantage of tree bark, burned or otherwise, is that the snow never completely covers it.

The elk rut, from early September through mid-October, is an exciting time. Bulls challenge each other for harems of 15 to 30 or more cows. At any time of day, you may hear bull elk asserting their dominance with loud calls or bugles. Battles include lots of rack-whacking, pushing, and wrestling, but they rarely end with serious injuries to either party.

Unlike other members of the deer family, bull elk keep their antlers during the winter to maintain social order. Elk winter in large gangs of mixed gender or males only. The bulls settle their disputes with few injuries, expending a minimum of energy. Without antlers, they would have to kick with their front hooves, as elk cows do when a predator attacks. Hooves can do real damage, and an injured elk might not make it through the winter. Sometime between mid-February and late March, bull elk shed their antlers and begin growing new sets.

As winter comes to an end, the herds move back to their summer ranges. Cows usually give birth to single spotted calves by late May or early June. Elk calves can walk within an hour of birth, but they spend most of their time

Elk outnumber all other grazing animals in the park. MIKE SAMPLE PHOTO

nursing and hiding from predators. Newborns weigh about 35 pounds (16 kg) and can gain 2 pounds (1 kg) a day during their first few weeks. A young bull begins growing his first set of antlers as a yearling, and is driven off by his mother at calving time.

Elk are the second largest members of the deer family (moose are the first). An average cow weighs more than 500 pounds (225 kg) and an average bull weighs 700 pounds (315 kg). The elk's brown coat darkens at the shoulders where a mane appears. The male's mane and large rack make him look a bit formidable. Elk also have distinctive light beige rump patches.

The Shawnee word for elk is *wapiti*, which means white-rumped deer. Europeans may prefer this term, since a smaller cousin of the moose lives in Europe and is called an elk.

Moose: The chocolate brown moose is the largest and homeliest member of the deer family. Its somewhat goofy and awkward "Bullwinkle" appearance belies its remarkable and well-functioning parts. Long legs enable the moose to feed on aquatic plants like water lilies and duckweed as it wades in ponds and rivers. Webbed cloven feet allow the moose to take the most direct route across a lake by swimming rather than circling the shoreline. A 6- to 10-inch (15–26 cm) flap of skin and hair hanging from the throat helps shed water as the moose lifts its head from a lake bottom. Large ears flap and wiggle, even while the moose sleeps, to pick up any hint of danger. When roused, the moose can move quickly and silently through the forest to safety.

Moose are solitary animals, getting together only during the rut (the mating season) from mid-September to late November. A male and female pair up for just a week or ten days before the bull moves on to another conquest. In early May, mature cows give birth to single calves. Moose mothers defend their babies with a vengeance. Cow moose are antlerless, but by using their sharp hooves, they can easily kill predators or any other animals they may perceive as threatening, including humans. An average cow weighs 675 pounds (300 kg).

Bull moose shed their antlers each year after the rut and begin growing new ones the following summer. Six weeks before breeding season begins again, they rub off the velvety outer skin, revealing new racks that may be 5 feet (1.5 m) across. Antlers are palmate, shaped like hands with fingers extended. Bull moose weigh an average of 900 pounds (400 kg). Both males and females live 18 to 20 years.

Moose are often seen munching aquatic plants, but their most important food source is woody browse plants like willow. Their dietary preference gave them their name: "moose" is derived from the Algonquin *musee* or "wood eater." In summer, look for moose feeding on willows around Swan Lake Flats, Willow Park, Soda Butte Creek, the Hayden and Pelican valleys, and the Lewis River.

In the winter, many of Yellowstone's several hundred moose migrate to lower elevations west and south of the park boundaries. Others move up, sometimes climbing to elevations of 8,500 feet (2,600 m) within the park, where they feed on the needles and twigs of subalpine fir and Douglas-fir. Snow gets caught in the thick canopies of these high-elevation fir stands, allowing the moose to move about easily on the ground below.

Pronghorns: The explorer William Clark is responsible for the continuing confusion over the name of this Great Plains animal. Clark accurately described the pronghorns he and other members of the Lewis and Clark Expedition observed, but he noted that the pronghorn "is more like the Antilope [sic] or Gazella [sic] of Africa than any other species of Goat [sic]." The pronghorn thus became known as an antelope, when it is actually the sole survivor of a different family of animals that evolved on this continent for 20 million years.

Clark compared the pronghorn to the gazelle in part because of its speed. The pronghorn is the fastest land animal in North America. At the first sign of danger, it bolts away at speeds of 45 to 50 miles per hour (72–80 kph). Small and otherwise vulnerable, the pronghorn relies on speed as its major defense against predation.

Oversized organs contribute to the pronghorns' speed, and help them survive in other ways, too. Pronghorns are able to outrun the fastest predators because their oversized windpipes carry extra oxygen to megalungs and because a greater-than-normal volume of blood is pumped through their extra-large hearts. Livers nearly twice the size proportionally of domestic sheep's filter toxins from vegetation that is unpalatable or poisonous to domestic livestock, allowing pronghorns to fully utilize a wider number of grasses and shrubs in their ranges. Large, protruding eyes provide pronghorns with an extraordinarily wide field of vision, helping them keep an eye out for danger.

Both male and female pronghorns stand about 3 feet (0.9 m) tall. Bucks weigh 100 to 125 pounds (50–62.5 kg) and does weigh 90 to 110 pounds (45–55 kg). Both have white bellies and rumps and distinctive white stripes across their throats. Bucks also have black cheek patches.

Pronghorns are the only animals with forked, or pronged, horns. These are "true" horns, with a sheath made of modified, fused hair that grows over a permanent bony core. Males shed these horny sheaths in November or December after the rut, and begin growing new ones for the following year. Nearly all the does have horns, but their horns are often hard to see because they are so small.

In winter, males and females band together in large herds of dozens or hundreds of animals. Come spring, they split into same-sex bands, though some older males go solo. Grayish brown twins, weighing 6.5 to 9 pounds (3.25–4.5 kg), are

And Others . . .

The park is rich with an abundance of other critters—from the tiniest brine fly hovering over the hot springs to the rare mountain lion stalking its prey. Yellowstone has the greatest concentration of large and small mammals in the lower 48 states.

Many animals scamper about in the daytime, but others go about their business under the cover of darkness. Wood rats, flying squirrels, and several kinds of mice are nocturnal. You can see chipmunks and golden-mantled ground squirrels at any time of day. The chipmunks are the ones with stripes on their sides and faces; the larger-bodied ground squirrels only have stripes on their sides.

Keep an eye out for "nature's plows" in open, grassy areas of the park. See if you can tell if freshly tilled soil is the work of ants, pocket gophers, or bears. The neat, round mounds are anthills. When pocket gophers cover up the openings to their tunnels, they leave lopsided mounds. Bears chasing after their fellow "plows" are anything but neat. As they dig for ants, food stored by pocket gophers, or the gophers themselves, bears leave rough tumbles of soil. If you come upon a meadow that looks totally topsy-turvy, a bear was probably at work there.

If you are very still, you can watch one mammal make a magical transformation: a rockchuck becomes a groundhog, then a woodchuck, then a whistle pig—just by moving from a rock to its burrow in the ground to the woods, where it gives a shrill, whistlelike call. Rockchuck, groundhog, woodchuck, and whistle pig are all names for the yellow-bellied marmot, a burrowing rodent with short ears and a short bushy tail.

In the open meadows of the park, watch for coyotes stalking mice, voles, and pocket gophers. You may also see them around hot springs, where they lie in wait to catch birds basking in the warmth or snacking on insects in the runoff channels. "Song dog" packs of a half-dozen of the German shepherd-like coyotes may prey on weak, very young, and very old deer and elk. Sometimes they just hang around a larger predator's kill and dart in for bites at opportune moments. The Park Service estimates that 450 coyotes in 65 packs patrol Yellowstone.

You probably won't see a mountain lion, or cougar, on your visit to the park, but 20 to 35 live here. These secretive predators stalk elk, deer, and pronghorns by night. In winter, mountain lions follow their prey to lower elevations, avoiding the deepest snows. Bobcats, lynx, and wolverines also live here and are just as seldom seen. Mountain goats, though not park natives, were introduced near the northwest and northeast corners of the park decades ago.

If you are a good observer, you may have the chance to see many other mammals (not to mention birds, fish, and insects) while you are in the park. Many animals are described in detail in those portions of the guide covering areas where you would most likely find them.

Even if you don't see a great variety of animals, it is nice just to know they are there. Remember, you are a visitor in their home, and you are always being watched—by someone or something.

born in May or June. Because of the pronghorns' wide-open habitat, the young are especially vulnerable to predators. At three weeks old, they can follow the does as they graze, but it is some time before they can keep up when a sentinel flashes its white rump and the herd dashes away from danger.

In the early 1800s, when pronghorns were second in number only to bison, 35 million roamed the West. By the 1920s, hunting, predation, and competition for range had whittled the herds to somewhere between 15,000 and 20,000 individuals. Today, careful management has increased that number to 500,000. Less than 250 pronghorns reside in the park.

Wolves: Unlike many of the animals in Yellowstone, gray wolves (also called timber wolves) live in families. A pack may have anywhere from two to ten members. It includes an alpha male and an alpha female, their offspring, and subordinate wolves. Each animal has a unique personality and plays a special role in pack life.

The pack communicates through facial expressions, body language, and scent-marking—urinating on shrubs and stumps. Wolves howl to locate members of their pack and to express their feelings of closeness to one another. They also howl to tell strange wolves to keep out of their territory, which they have carefully scent-marked.

The largest wild member of the dog family, a mature male wolf weighs 95 to 100 pounds (43–45 kg) and measures as much as 3 feet (0.9 m) high at the shoulder. Female wolves, or bitches, weigh 80 to 85 pounds (36–38 kg) and are about 2.5 feet (0.75 m) tall. Pups are born blind, deaf, and furred, and weigh about 1 pound (0.5 kg). Only the alpha male and alpha female mate, but the whole pack is kept busy feeding the litter of four to eight pups. An adult may consume up to 20 pounds (9.1 kg) of meat each day so that it can regurgitate some to feed the wolf brood.

Coyotes (another member of the dog family and also park residents) can live on bugs and berries, but wolves only eat meat. Although Farley Mowatt's book (which was also made into a movie) *Never Cry Wolf* portrays wolves living on mice alone, they can't survive without the bigger meals that pronghorns, deer, and elk provide. The wolf pack chases a herd, and when one member falls behind—usually one that is weak, young, or old—the wolves close in for the kill. In this way, the wolves actually help strengthen the ungulate population, since the strongest animals most often survive to pass on their genes to the next generation. Because wolves kill regularly, they also provide carrion for other animals such as red foxes, wolverines, coyotes, weasels, and birds.

After an absence of more than 60 years, the gray wolf was returned to the Greater Yellowstone Ecosystem in 1995. To learn why this significant predator was missing and how it was reintroduced, see page 94 of the guide's "Northeast Entrance to Tower-Roosevelt Junction" section.

Getting to Know Yellowstone

It is impossible to get to know Yellowstone through the windows of your car, bus, camper, or snowcoach. Get out of that moving cocoon and hike or ski the trails as often as you can. Smell the pines, the sulfur, and the wet earth. As you walk along the paths and boardwalks of the thermal areas, feel the heat from the steaming hot springs and the wind-blown spray from the geysers. Hear the ravens' cries, the thunderous roar of water as it crashes down from the brink of a waterfall, the splattering and gurgling of the mud pots, and the chatter of golden-mantled ground squirrels.

Offered throughout the summer, ranger-naturalist talks in the park's amphitheaters will help you understand more about Yellowstone. Pick up maps and information from visitor centers everywhere you go. Try to join a ranger-naturalist for a special walk, ski, or daytime program. Kids ages five to twelve can become Junior Rangers by completing activities explained in a mini-newspaper sold at visitor centers. Each year, more than 11,000 children earn their Junior Ranger patches.

Be a Smart Park Visitor

Remember, you are in a wild place where everything is in as natural a state as possible. This means there are special rules to follow for a safe and low-impact visit:

Take only photographs and memories. Every national park, including Yellowstone, prohibits the possession, removal, or destruction of any plant, mineral, or animal. So don't pick any flowers, pocket any rocks, or snatch up any dropped antlers. It is the law!

Stay on the boardwalks and trails. Each year, visitors fall through the thin crusts around thermal features; some receive second- or third-degree burns; others die. Remember: "better safe than sorry." Even if you are not injured, your one step could destroy hundreds of years of fragile hot springs deposits.

All thermal features are out-of-bounds for swimming or soaking. In certain locations, where the runoff empties into a river or lake, you may take a dip. Ask a park ranger first.

No smoking in thermal areas! Aside from the unsightly litter of cigarette butts that accumulates wherever smoking is permitted, live ashes could light up sulfur deposits, which would then release dangerous and perhaps lethal gases. Smoking is hazardous to your health anyway. Here, it could be deadly.

Leave your pets at home, or at least in the car. Dogs don't always stop to check if the water is hot or cold. Given the opportunity, they may jump into a hot pool to cool off. Not only will dogs die or receive severe burns, but people will, too, if they attempt to rescue their pets. Dogs also disturb wildlife. For these reasons, park rules prohibit pets on all boardwalks and trails throughout the park.

Do not feed the animals. Food attracts bears and other mammals to campgrounds, so make sure yours is properly stowed. That means keeping your campsite clean and locking food in your car. In the backcountry, hang your food 10 feet (3 m) above the ground and 5 feet (1.5 m) away from a post or tree trunk. If food is left where bears can get to it, both bears and people are at risk. Park policy is to remove offending bears. If bears become repeat offenders and threaten human safety, they may be destroyed.

Although the animals you see appear calm and accustomed to visitors pointing cameras at them, every one of them is wild and potentially dangerous. A bull elk, moose, bison, or bear calmly "posing" for a picture could charge you in an instant. And a tiny ground squirrel begging to share your lunch might just share a disease with you, too. Park regulations require you *to stay at least 100 yards (90 m) away from bears and at least 25 yards (22.5 m) away from all other animals* to avoid harassing them.

Watch all animals from a safe distance, or better yet, from your vehicle. Use binoculars or a telephoto lens to ensure safe viewing. *If your presence causes an animal to move, you are too close.* In the winter, when conserving energy is so crucial to wild animals, extra stress could mean the difference between life and death.

Elevation and weather changes can be extreme. Park elevation ranges from 5,282 feet (1,585 m) at Reese Creek near the North Entrance to 11,358 feet (3,463 m) at the summit of Eagle Peak in the park's southeast corner. If you have come from a much lower elevation to visit Yellowstone, you will probably find that you tire easily and dehydrate more quickly in the thin, dry air. *Pace yourself and drink lots of fluids,* especially in the winter.

Whether it is summer or winter, a day that starts out sunny can quickly turn nasty, so always *wear clothing in layers* and be prepared for driving rain or howling blizzards. Average temperatures range from 0 degrees F (-18°C) in January to 76 degrees F (24°C) in August.

Be prepared for emergencies on the trail. Carry extra clothing, food, water, matches, a first-aid kit, and, if you are skiing or snowmobiling, a repair kit.

Winter's extremely cold temperatures present obvious hazards. From mid-December to early March, skiers and snowmobilers can find refuge in 24 warming huts located at Indian Creek, Madison Junction, Old Faithful, West Thumb, Fishing Bridge, and Canyon Junction. All but the Indian Creek hut have telephone service.

Permits are required for all vessels, whether they are motor boats or float tubes. Boaters and floaters can get permits at the South Entrance, Lewis Lake Campground, Grant Village Visitor Center, Bridge Bay Marina, or Lake Ranger Station. No boating is allowed on the park's rivers, except in the Lewis River Channel, where only nonmotorized craft may be used.

Backcountry permits are required for all overnight hikes and some day treks. Visiting the backcountry on foot, skis, horseback, or canoe is a special way to get to know Yellowstone, but backcountry travel also presents special hazards. Encounters with bears and other large animals are more frequent in the backcountry. Extremely cold, deep water and the possibility of sudden storms present problems that boaters and anglers should consider. For more information, ask a park ranger, or write to Backcountry Office, P.O. Box 168, Yellowstone National Park, Wyoming 82190.

If you obey park regulations and follow the above precautions, walking across the highway might be the most dangerous thing you do during your visit to Yellowstone. Remember, though, that under no circumstance can your safety be guaranteed.

Fishing

Fishing is an anomaly in Yellowstone National Park. While park policy prevents the harvest of other animals, trees, or minerals, fishing has been a major visitor activity since the park's founding. To guard against over-consumption by human anglers, park regulations limit the size and number of fish you can take, specify what fishing tackle you can use, and, in some places, impose catch-and-release restrictions. In every case, the needs of wild anglers like bald eagles, ospreys, pelicans, otters, and grizzly bears take precedence.

State fishing licenses are not required in Yellowstone, but anglers aged 16 and older must purchase park fishing permits, and those aged 12 to 15 must have free park permits in their possession. Younger children do not need permits, but adults who know park rules must accompany them. Permits for ten days or for the entire season are available at all visitor centers, ranger stations, and general stores.

With some exceptions, Yellowstone's fishing season runs from the Saturday of Memorial Day weekend through the first Sunday of November. Generally, fishing on Yellowstone Lake opens June 15, and the Yellowstone River and its tributaries between Chittenden Bridge and Yellowstone Lake (except for the Hayden Valley) open for fishing on July 15. Hayden Valley, the Grand Canyon of the Yellowstone River, and other areas are permanently closed to fishing. For more information, refer to park fishing regulations.

Access for People with Disabilities

People with permanent disabilities are eligible for Golden Access Passports, which provide free lifetime entrance to federal parks, historic sites, and recreation areas where entrance fees are charged. The passports also allow free entry to all passengers in the passport holder's private vehicle. Discounts on federal use fees are also available.

Within funding constraints, the National Park Service continues to work toward providing wheelchair access to as many of Yellowstone's features and facilities as possible. Contact the National Park Service Accessibility Coordinator, P.O. Box 168, Yellowstone National Park, Wyoming 82190; 307-344-2018 or TDD 307-344-2386.

Trails

Yellowstone is laced with trails for hiking and cross-country skiing. This guide includes many short and easy hikes or skis for families; a few longer ones are also included for adults or families with older children. For more ideas on where to hike or ski in Yellowstone, see *Best Easy Day Hikes: Yellowstone* (Falcon Publishing, $6.95), *Yellowstone Trails: A Hiking Guide* by Mark C. Marschall (The Yellowstone Association, $4.95), or *Yellowstone Winter Guide* by Jeff Henry (Roberts Rinehart, $11.95). Wherever you go, please take along a plastic sack to pick up litter left behind by less-thoughtful visitors.

One trail you might consider is the Howard Eaton Trail. This 157-mile (251.2 km) trail roughly parallels the Grand Loop Road, a rough figure eight that leads to the primary points of interest throughout the park. You can hike bits and pieces of the trail to catch the flavor of park travel "off the beaten path." You will find Howard Eaton trailheads scattered throughout the park, including one at the Old Faithful Ranger Station, one at the Beaver Ponds trailhead at Mammoth Hot Springs, and one at the parking lot east of Fishing Bridge. Watch for two other Howard Eaton trailheads along the bar of the figure eight: one is 3.5 miles (5.6 km) east of Norris Geyser Basin, and the other is 0.5 mile (0.8 km) west of Canyon Junction. This parkwide trail honors outfitter Howard Eaton, who offered horse trips that followed a similar route from 1885 to 1921.

a family guide to
YELLOWSTONE NATIONAL PARK

Yellowstone has more than 300 miles (480 km) of paved roads. The Grand Loop Road, which crosses the Continental Divide twice at an average elevation of 7,500 to 8,000 feet (2,250–2,400 m), takes up nearly half the road miles.

You can forget trying to figure mileage in terms of hours. Although the speed limit is 45 miles per hour (73 kph) throughout most of the park, "animal jams," narrow roads, and road construction will undo any notion you might have of getting from Point A to Point B in X amount of time. The combination of daily earth tremors and radical freezing and thawing causes no end of potholes, frost heaves, and road maintenance crews to appear throughout this high country. Delays are not only possible—in some areas, they are certain. If time is of the essence, call the park for road information before you arrive.

Each of the five paved entrances is unique. Only two are open year-round: the North and Northeast entrances. During the winter, the Northeast Entrance Road extends only about 10 miles (16 km) beyond the park boundary to Cooke City, Montana. The other entrances are closed to wheeled vehicles throughout the winter, which may extend to Memorial Day weekend.

How to Use This Guide

To begin your journey, find the name of the park entrance you will use in the Table of Contents. Then follow along section by section as you travel around the park. Each section contains bits of information to help make your visit a fun-filled learning experience. Throughout the guide, **bold-faced type** highlights significant natural and manmade features in the Greater Yellowstone Ecosystem. *Italicized notes* list the facilities you will find at major points of interest in summer and in winter. Now, come along, and let's explore Yellowstone National Park together!

West Entrance to Madison Junction

14 miles (23 km)
Elevation at West Entrance: 6,667 feet (2,032 m)

⊛ *The **West Entrance Road** is closed to wheeled motorized vehicles from about the first Monday in November to the third Friday in April.*
Facilities at the West Entrance: None.

Entering the park on the outskirts of **West Yellowstone, Montana,** you follow the trail of early Indians, trappers, prospectors, explorers, and stagecoaches down the broad, flat **Madison River Valley.** River erosion and ancient glacial activity made this valley and others natural choices as sites for the trails and roads throughout Yellowstone's mountainous country. The **West Entrance Road** roughly parallels the gently meandering **Madison River** as it enters the state of **Wyoming.**

Meriwether Lewis and William Clark named the river in 1805 after our fourth president, James Madison. When President Thomas Jefferson commissioned the Lewis and Clark Expedition to explore the West, James Madison was secretary of state. Lewis and Clark never saw this portion of the Madison River, though they camped downstream for several days near what is now the community of **Three Forks** in south-central Montana. There, the Madison joins the **Gallatin and Jefferson rivers** to form the mighty **Missouri River.**

The West Entrance Road is a path through a seemingly never-ending corridor of lodgepole pines, but only for the first 2 to 3 miles (3.2–4.8 km). After that, only the skeletal frame of the corridor remains, a blackened reminder of the North Fork fire of 1988. The fire burned hot and fast along both sides of the road and the river. At one point, it threatened the gateway community of West Yellowstone. The aftermath of the fire treats travelers to a clear view of terrain that was once concealed by the walls of trees. Sporadic glacial boulders, precipitous cliffs, and grassy knolls are now visible. Young lodgepole pines once again crowd each other on the valley floor.

Take a break at any pullout along the river and stretch your legs or, about 5 miles (8 km) east of the West Entrance, stop at a wayside exhibit and follow **Two Ribbons Trail,** an easy 1.5-mile (2.4 km) boardwalk along the Madison River. From the boardwalk, you can see how the land has recovered from the 1988 fires. Also look for spots where bison wallow, or roll around, in the soft sand. Children can easily spot minnows and aquatic insects in the lazy river.

Why are there so many big boulders in the river? Look at the hills around you and imagine standing on this spot during the **Hebgen Lake** earthquake, centered just 12 miles (19.2 km) north of West Yellowstone along

Exotic Species Threaten Yellowstone's Blue Ribbon Streams

Falling boulders created a special type of habitat in the **Madison River** and continue to help the river qualify as one of America's blue-ribbon trout streams. However, exotic species now threaten this world-class fishery.

In local areas along the Madison, **Firehole** and **Gibbon Rivers**, the New Zealand mud snail is displacing native aquatic invertebrate communities, a critical part of the aquatic food chain. Portions of the Madison riverbed, in fact, are covered with 28,000 individuals per square inch. These tiny black snails, measuring less than 0.25 inch (6.35 mm), are crowding out native invertebrates such as mayflies, stoneflies, and caddis flies, and out-competing them for food. Biologists say the mud snails are a poor nutritional substitute for fish.

Park scientists suspect humans inadvertently introduced mud snails since these prolific invertebrates are able to withstand desiccation and a wide range of temperatures, and are small enough to be transported undetected by anglers, swimmers, picnickers, and pets.

A parasitic malady also threatens Yellowstone's blue-ribbon fisheries. Whirling disease is caused by a microscopic parasite that completes part of its life cycle in the aquatic tubifex worm and then attacks the cartilage forming the spines of young trout and salmon. The resulting deformities cause these fish to swim in endless circles, making it hard for them to feed normally or evade predators.

Whirling disease took its toll on what was once a world-class fishery just outside Yellowstone, south of **Hebgen Lake.** In 1994, after watching the trout population decline drastically over the preceding three years, biologists confirmed the presence of whirling disease in the upper Madison River drainage. Fortunately, the clear, deep holes and free-stone gravelly beds of the Madison River and other streams and rivers inside Yellowstone have historically kept those waters free of disease.

In 1998, however, biologists found whirling disease, for the first time in the park, in fish living in a tributary of **Yellowstone Lake.** While whirling disease undoubtedly has spread to the lake's other tributaries, so far the only fish that have tested positive have been adults, which appear to have survived the onset of the disease without serious harm.

To help prevent the spread of New Zealand mud snails and the tubifex worms that host whirling disease, the Park Service urges anglers to clean mud, plants, and debris from fishing equipment and to inspect footwear before leaving their fishing sites. Further, anglers should drain creels and only clean fish in the body of water where they are caught; mud snail locations should be reported to a park ranger.

the western edge of the park. The 1959 temblor knocked loose a lot of boulders that moving, melting glaciers had left scattered around the valley walls eons before. Some of these huge rocks landed in the Madison River and created deep holes where brown and rainbow trout can now rest and feed.

Autumn is a good time to spot a bull elk with his harem on the Madison River. MIKE SAMPLE PHOTO

Seven miles (11.2 km) east of the West Entrance is **Seven Mile Bridge,** where you may see graceful, all-white trumpeter swans on the water or on the bridge's floating nesting platform.

One of our country's greatest conservation efforts focused on the trumpeter swan, and essayist and novelist E. B. White wrote a prize-winning children's novel, *The Trumpet of the Swan,* about the great birds. Like White's protagonist, Louis the Swan, these large waterfowl have wingspans of 8 feet (2.4 m), but they don't need brass trumpets to make their sonorous, trumpeting calls.

Please keep your distance from these graceful birds. They require undisturbed territory to raise their young cygnets.

Seven Mile Bridge is also an excellent place to watch fish any time of year. If you approach the railing slowly and quietly, you may see several large trout resting upstream between banks of weeds. Trout thrive here even in midwinter because thermal runoff keeps the Madison River at a tolerable 50 degrees F (10°C). The warmth allows aquatic plants and algae to produce life-giving oxygen and provide the trout with a nonstop banquet of various insects.

The Madison River Valley is an especially crucial winter range for 650 to 850 elk in the Firehole-Madison herd and about 1,300 to 1,400 bison in the Mary Mountain-Firehole herd. The Firehole-Madison elk are year-round residents of Yellowstone Park. They spend the winters near thermal areas, where high-quality forage plants grow. In the summer, you might see brown-headed cowbirds picking insects and ticks off the backs of their bison pals.

Just before the West Entrance Road meets the **Grand Loop Road,** you will see the **Gibbon and Firehole rivers** rushing in from the east and south to form the Madison River. This is the northern boundary of the **Yellowstone Caldera.**

Trumpeter Swans

· ·

At one time, trumpeter swans nested and fed by the thousands in this hemisphere, from the Arctic down to the Gulf Coast and from the Pacific Ocean eastward to the marshes of Indiana and northern Missouri. Then, in the early 1800s, the fashion world discovered the trumpeters. People began to demand the swans' pure white feathers and soft down for decorations and powder puffs; gourmets ate the trumpeters' eggs. It is even said that the famed artist and naturalist John J. Audubon favored the primary feathers of trumpeter swans for his writing quills.

Fur companies handled as many as 2,000 swanskins a year. They sold most of the skins in England, though many Americans also followed the whims of fashion. Despite the vast numbers of swans, market hunting and the disturbance it created devastated the species.

When Yellowstone National Park was created in 1872, it provided a partial sanctuary for the trumpeters, but poachers continued to decimate resident birds. Finally, in 1912, the remaining population of trumpeter swans received protection from the Migratory Bird Act. Yet 20 years later, scientists could only find 69 trumpeters in the continental United States. A Yellowstone biologist at **Red Rock Lakes, Montana,** just west of the park boundary, discovered the swans. In 1935, Congress created the 40,000-acre (16,000 ha) **Red Rock Lakes National Wildlife Refuge,** and the last trumpeters were fed grain and carefully protected. Slowly they began to rebuild their flocks.

Today the Red Rocks area is home to between 500 and 600 year-round-resident swans and more than a thousand winter migrants (plus, of course, Louis the Swan). Fifteen pairs sometimes nest in the park in summer. Look for them along the Madison River and at **Swan Lake,** south of **Mammoth Hot Springs** and **Golden Gate.**

Madison Junction to Old Faithful

. . . .

16 miles (26 km)
Elevation at Madison Junction: 6,806 feet (2,091 m)

✿ *Summer facilities at Madison Junction: museum, information station and bookstore, amphitheater, campground. Winter facilities: warming hut, daytime snack bar, vending machines.*

AmFac Parks & Resorts has the campground concession at the headwaters of the **Madison River.** This site has provided campers with abundant fish and wildlife, water, safety, and access to park wonders for thousands of years. Ancient people, fur trappers, prospectors, and even the Nez Perce in their 1877 flight from the Army, found shelter here among the lodgepole pines. A Park Service ranger-naturalist is often at the campground, ready to answer questions about this area of the park.

The Washburn-Langford-Doane expedition of 1870 spent its last night in Yellowstone on a point of land between the **Gibbon and Firehole rivers** south of **Madison Junction.** The **Madison Museum** occupies the Wash-burn campsite and once celebrated the genesis of the national park movement. No longer a museum, the building houses an information station and a Yellowstone Association bookstore. The peeled-log and stone construction of the Madison Museum and the **Norris Geyser Basin Museum,** both built in 1929, became prototypes for "parkitecture" throughout the United States. Designed to be part of, not apart from, their environment, both museums are

Fish in Hot Water

. . . .

Thermal features make the **Firehole River** a blue-ribbon trout stream with a difference. Hot springs and geysers boost its temperature to as high as 86 degrees F (30°C) in some places. Yet the Firehole supports lively populations of native Yellowstone cutthroat trout and rainbow, brown, and brook trout, three species that were "planted" in the river a century ago.

For a trout, 67 degrees F (19°C) is the ideal temperature. So when thermal water temperatures get too high, the trout leave the "kitchen" for cooler tributary streams. Unnaturally hot water, like that produced by power plants and some industries, can wreak havoc in a fish population, killing fish outright or causing diseases and impeding life cycles. But when hot water is a part of their natural environment, fish and other aquatic organisms learn to cope—naturally.

Learn about nature through immersion at the Firehole River. MIKE SAMPLE PHOTO

recognized as National Historic Landmarks. Across the Firehole River, **National Park Mountain** commemorates the birth of the national park idea.

Keep an eye out for red-tailed hawks and three-toed woodpeckers. Around dusk, you might spot a common nighthawk cruising the open meadows.

The **Grand Loop Road** parallels the Firehole River through an area park road-builder Hiram Chittenden described as the "home of the genus geyser, as seen in its highest development." The river's name was borrowed from another waterway that coursed through a scorched valley west of the park, the "Fire Hole" or "Burnt Hole." (In trapper parlance, "hole" meant a mountain valley.) In the 1830s, trappers easily transferred the name to the present Firehole River, since it also described the thermal features found here. Indeed, this Firehole River is probably the river that mountain man Jim Bridger allegedly claimed ran so fast that it got hot on the bottom. Hot springs actually warm the river near its banks and below the water's surface as it runs north through the geyser basins. You'll have to admit, all that steam rising from the river would make a mountain man wonder what in tarnation was going on!

Beyond the bridge and information station, **Firehole Canyon Drive** winds upstream through **Firehole Canyon.** The 2-mile (3.2 km), one-way (south) drive traces an old Indian trail along the river, cutting through volcanic rhyolite from the Yellowstone volcano of 600,000 years ago. The power of erosion is evident here. The road passes between 800-foot (240 m) black lava walls and affords a close-up view of **Firehole Falls** with its 40-foot (12 m) drop. Watch for American dippers plying the swift current. Upriver from the falls is a well-marked but unstaffed swimming area. As the river sliced this deep canyon, it broke off chunks of rhyolite rubble which created deep holes in the riverbed. If it is hot, you may feel like swimming. Be careful in the fast moving water, and no cliff diving!

Beyond the swimming hole, Firehole Canyon Drive rejoins the Grand Loop Road. Here, the white, churning water of the **Firehole Cascades** rushes past grassy banks and more dead-standing tree ghosts from the fires of 1988. The water tumbles over the steep rocks, then smoothes out again. Watch for prehistoric-looking great blue herons wading in the slower water, stalking the wily trout.

A couple of miles south of the cascades, you will enter the 12-square-mile (19.2 km²) **Lower Geyser Basin,** the largest geyser basin in Yellowstone National Park. The 1871 Hayden survey officially counted 680 geysers here. Today's park personnel may not be able to estimate how many geysers are active on any given day, so let's just say there are a lot of them out there. Some will probably spout during your visit.

Because Lower Geyser Basin is north of the other geyser basins on the west side of Yellowstone, you might wonder why it isn't called Upper Geyser Basin. The answer is that the Firehole River flows north, so Lower Geyser Basin is actually downstream from the other basins.

Eight miles (12.9 km) from both Madison Junction and **Old Faithful** is the entrance to **Fountain Flat Drive,** an old freight road that runs behind Lower and **Midway geyser basins.** In summer, the road is closed to motorized vehicles at the 1-mile (1.6 km) mark. Bike and foot traffic are allowed over the next 4 miles (6.4 km). Fountain Flat Drive rejoins the Grand Loop Road south of Midway Geyser Basin.

Fountain Flat Drive will take you to several park features including **Ojo Caliente** (Spanish for "hot spring") **Springs** in **Sentinel Meadows.** The stands of aspen and willows in these open meadows provide habitat for a number of bird species, including the red-crowned sandhill crane. Listen for its rattly call in the morning or early evening and watch for this long-legged gray bird feasting on insects, frogs, rodents, and vegetation. Like trumpeter swans and other birds and mammals in the park, cranes require peace and quiet, so please watch them from a distance.

On the west side of Sentinel Meadows is the **Queen's Laundry,** a once active hot spring where early park workers washed their clothes and bathed. Thermal changes and vandalism have taken their toll, and the hot spring, with its brightly colored terraces, is gone.

In winter, you can ski the length of Fountain Flat Drive. A snowcoach will also drop off skiers at the trailhead to **Fairy Falls** for an 11-mile (17.6

km) ski back to Old Faithful. Along the way, watch for herds of bison bedded down on the warmed earth of the thermal areas, conserving their own energy. Fountain Flat is a favorite bison haunt in the cold winter months.

Right after the turnoff to Fountain Flat Drive, the Grand Loop Road crosses the Firehole River near its confluence with **Nez Perce Creek.** The creek was named to commemorate the trek of five bands of nontreaty Nez Perce Indians across the park, with the Army in pursuit. Near this spot on August 23 and 24, 1877, the Nez Perce took their first white hostages: a luckless prospector and ten tourists from Radersburg, Montana. By August 25, seven of the tourists had escaped, though some of them were wounded. The Nez Perce released the rest of their group near the **Mud Volcano,** just north of **Yellowstone Lake.** The prospector escaped a week later, after helping guide the Nez Perce through the Yellowstone area.

Look for elk and bison grazing in the meadows along Nez Perce Creek. But please watch them from a distance. Each year, as many as ten park visitors are seriously hurt because they get too close, forgetting that the calm-looking beasts are wild.

Proceeding south on the Grand Loop Road, you will see low, rounded hills to the east. These remnants of the ice age in Yellowstone are glacial moraines—mounds of rock and rubble that the rivers of ice picked up and carried along, then laid down again as the glaciers melted.

South of the turnoff to Fountain Flat Drive and Nez Perce Creek, you can stop and take a 0.5-mile (0.8 km) walk among the **Fountain Paint Pots,** one of the largest groups of mud pots in the park. Here, you will see examples of each of Yellowstone's thermal features—geysers, hot springs, mud pots, and fumaroles. As you walk along the boardwalk, notice how underground water helps create the various geothermal features. Near the foot of the hill, the water collects in the heavenly **Celestine Pool** and **Silex Spring.** Silex Spring is so full it overflows a broad area, creating a restricted environment for mats of bacteria that thrive in hot water. Silex is Latin for silica, the mineral discharged by these thermal features.

Farther up the boardwalk is **Clepsydra Geyser,** which plays almost continuously at heights of 20 to 33 feet (6–10 m). In 1873, Theodore Comstock named the geyser because "like the ancient water-clock of that name, it marks the passage of time by the discharge of water." Several small geysers spout near Clepsydra, including **Twig, Morning, Red Spouter, Fountain, Jet, Spasm,** and **Jelly.** Up the hill, water becomes less plentiful, but it is ample enough to supply the bubbling Fountain Paint Pots and **Leather Pool.** Depending on the season and recent precipitation, these pots may appear thin and watery or thick as mud. At the very top of the hill, where water is really in short supply, only fumaroles, or steam vents, are active.

Explore the Fountain Paint Pots for an introduction to Yellowstone's geothermal features.
MIKE SNYDER PHOTO

Farther south on the Grand Loop Road, you will come to **Firehole Lake Drive.** This 3-mile (4.8 km), one-way (north) road leads first to **Great Fountain Geyser,** one of the most magnificent geysers in the world. Great Fountain erupts every 11 to 15 hours for 45 to 60 minutes. On average, it spouts 115 feet (34.5 m) in the air, but it can go as high as 200 feet (60 m).

In 1869, Great Fountain shot steam and water skyward just as the Folsom-Cook-Peterson party entered the Lower Geyser Basin for the first time. These men had come a long way to see if the tall tales and rumors they had heard were true. One of the explorers, Charles W. Cook, later wrote: "We could not contain our enthusiasm; with one accord we all took off our hats and yelled with all our might."

Farther along Firehole Lake Drive, **White Dome Geyser** erupts almost hourly to heights of 23 to 30 feet (7–9 m). **Pink Cone** is also active and fairly dependable.

Another major feature on this short drive is **Firehole Lake,** a large hot spring with an average temperature of 158 degrees F (70°C). Across the road and downhill from Firehole Lake, take a steamy walk around **Steady Geyser** and **Hot Lake.** Hot Lake is the collecting basin for runoff from Steady Geyser and Firehole Lake.

Firehole Lake Drive leads back to the Grand Loop Road, which soon brings you to Midway Geyser Basin. A bridge across the Firehole River leads to the basin's major features. Midway Basin is small, almost totally confined to a narrow strip of land along a 1-mile (1.6 km) stretch of the river, but its features are spectacular. Midway Basin contains only seven geysers of any size, yet it is the site of two of the world's largest hot springs. **Grand Prismatic Spring** is more than 370 by 120 feet (111 x 36 m). The crater of **Excelsior Geyser** measures about 200 by 300 feet (60 x 90 m).

The immense size of Grand Prismatic Spring and the patriotic colors reflected in its steam caught the eye of trapper Osbourne Russell in 1839. The water vapor that rose from "Boiling Lake," Russell wrote in his journal, "was of three distinct Colors [;] from the west side for one third of the diameter it was white, in the middle it was pale red, and the remaining third on the east light sky blue." He observed further that "the water was of deep indigo blue boiling like an imense [sic] cauldron running over the white rock which had formed [around] the edges to the height of 4 or 5 feet from the surface of the earth sloping gradually for 60 or 70 feet." Compare Russell's observations with your own. How has the spring changed?

Excelsior is Latin for higher, and the Excelsior Geyser used to be the largest in the world. After its last recorded eruption in 1891, it went dormant for nearly a hundred years. But it continued to leak nearly 5.8 million gallons (22 million l) of boiling water a day into the Firehole River below. Then, on September 14, 1985, Excelsior blasted to life in 47 straight hours of violent explosions. "Hell's Half-Acre" afterwards resumed its placid appearance. It has since produced the same amount of daily runoff as before—enough to fill more than 200 railroad tank cars or more than 300,000 automobile gas tanks!

Firehole Lake Drive leads to several active geysers, including Pink Cone. MIKE SNYDER PHOTO

One mile (1.6 km) south of Midway Geyser Basin, the Grand Loop Road meets the trail from the end of Fountain Flat Drive. Leave your car in the convenient parking lot and cross **Soldier Bridge** for a flat 1-mile (1.6 km) walk to the Fairy Falls trailhead. With a drop of 200 feet (60 m), Fairy Falls is one of Yellowstone's highest and most accessible waterfalls. In summer, the walk to the trailhead will probably offer you glimpses of mountain bluebirds nesting in the burned-over forest, and northern flickers and hairy woodpeckers drilling into the dead and dying trees. The falls are another 1.6 miles (2.6 km) from the trailhead. From the parking lot, the round-trip distance of 5.2 miles (8.3 km) is a bit long for little hikers, but rewarding for bigger ones. You can also get to Fairy Falls from the trailhead at the end of Fountain Flat Drive, which runs behind Grand Prismatic Spring and rejoins the Grand Loop Road at the Soldier Bridge parking lot.

A half-mile (0.8 km) south of the parking lot at the exit from Fountain Flat Drive, the Grand Loop enters a lodgepole pine forest. In winter, look for bull bison and cow elk around warm-water springs. As the road approaches **Biscuit Basin,** watch for bull elk.

If you cross the footbridge at Biscuit Basin, you might see violet-green swallows cruising low over the Firehole River in search of insects. The basin was named for the biscuitlike geyserite formations that once surrounded **Sapphire Pool.** When the vivid blue pool briefly erupted after the 1959 earthquake, most of the biscuits were washed into the river.

At the back of the basin, near **Avoca Spring,** a 2.4-mile (3.8 km) round-trip trail leads to **Mystic Falls,** a 70-foot (21 m) drop in the **Little Firehole**

River. Take the right fork and hike or ski along the river. This moderately difficult trail cuts through a lodgepole pine forest, then follows a series of switchbacks to the top of the falls. The scenic view encompasses the falls' sheeting water as well as Biscuit and Upper geyser basins. From Old Faithful, the round-trip distance to Mystic Falls is about 7 miles (11.2 km).

Just 1.5 miles (2.2 km) beyond Biscuit Basin, the Grand Loop Road passes **Black Sand Basin,** named for its sandy black carpet of ground obsidian (volcanic glass). Black Sand Basin is known for its splendid, colorful hot springs, and for **Cliff Geyser,** on the edge of **Iron Spring Creek.** Cliff Geyser frequently erupts 25 to 33 feet in the air (8–10 m) for several hours at a time.

Brace yourself. As you approach Old Faithful and the **Upper Geyser Basin,** the Grand Loop Road suddenly becomes a four-lane divided highway with a cloverleaf interchange. Since Old Faithful is the most popular, most visited place in the park, the immediate area has been paved over to accommodate heavy traffic. The good news is that, for the most part, the masses of people concentrate in the vicinity of Old Faithful (the geyser), near the trappings of civilization. Finding a place to park can be frustrating, but rest assured that once you stow your car or snowmobile, you can find peace if you are willing to walk a little.

Old Faithful to West Thumb

17 miles (27 km)
Elevation at Old Faithful: 7,365 feet (2,254 m)

⭐ *Year-round facilities at Old Faithful: visitor center, ranger station, clinic, lodging, food service, general store.* **Summer-only facilities:** *ranger station, auditorium, post office, photo shop, service station, auto repair, public showers.* **Winter-only facilities:** *warming hut, snowmobile fuel.*

The **Old Faithful** area has more geysers concentrated within just 1 square mile (2.59 km²) than any other geyser basin in the world. In fact, the 150 geysers of the **Upper Geyser Basin** represent more than a quarter of the world's total number of geysers. Because of this renowned thermal richness, the Upper Geyser Basin is a tourist mecca. At any given moment, several of the geysers could show their stuff!

If you are in the park between June and September, stop at the information desk at the **Old Faithful Visitor Center.** Here, ranger-naturalists post their educated guesses—within a ten-minute margin of error—as to the time of the most popular and regular geysers' next eruptions. Remember, these

Old Faithful's frequent eruptions always draw a captive audience. MIKE SAMPLE PHOTO

Probing the Earth's Interior

The hot water—3,700 to 8,400 gallons (14,000–32,000 l) of it—that **Old Faithful** sends skyward with each eruption moves faster than the speed of sound, according to James Westphal, an astronomer and modern-day explorer.

In 1992, Westphal and a team of scientists from the California Institute of Technology lowered a video camera into Old Faithful's narrow vent to investigate its recharge. Between eruptions, the camera explored a mysterious maze of underground channels and, at one point, revealed a 200- to 600-year-old tree wedged deep in Old Faithful's vent. As the geyser repeated its timeless process of recharging, the camera showed silica-charged water boiling 47 feet (14.1 m) below the earth's surface. The boiling point at that particular elevation is 199 degrees F (93°C). The camera plunged to a final depth of 68 feet (20.4 m), which was as far as it could go in the time allowed.

Westphal's investigation of Old Faithful's inner workings showed that the geyser draws groundwater from its side channels, which in turn are fed by precipitation that collects in the **Upper Geyser Basin.** Comparing surface water with water in the geyser's complex plumbing system, Westphal determined that much of the water in the underground reservoir was at least 20 years old. The proof was in the water's slight radioactivity from atomic testing in Nevada at least two decades earlier.

Other experiments revealed that the temperature of the water rushing from the geyser's vent is 204 degrees F (95.6°C)—30 degrees F (1°C) colder than the steam accompanying it.

Westphal and his colleagues solved the problem of filming in a turbulent, mineralized, hot-water world by placing their camera in a double-walled vacuum thermos (similar to one you may carry to school or work) and securing the whole thing with duct tape.

are only predictions. The Park Service has an unofficial motto: "We just predict, we do not schedule."

Without a doubt, Old Faithful is the world's best-known geyser. It has been the symbol of Yellowstone since the park was established in 1872, just two years after the geyser was christened by the Washburn expedition. While other geysers in Yellowstone spout more predictably, have larger cones, or throw up higher columns of water and steam, Old Faithful continues to live up to its name. Since the geyser was discovered, vandalism and powerful earthquakes have only slightly stretched the intervals between its eruptions. Because of its resiliency and blessed regularity, Old Faithful is probably the most studied geyser in the world.

The vastness and variety of the Upper Basin's geysers largely inspired the effort to preserve Yellowstone as a national park. When explorers in the 1870s came upon what some likened to a "manufacturing center," they christened many of the basin's thermal features, choosing names that "best illustrate[d] their peculiarities," according to Nathaniel Langford of the Washburn expedition. Early photographers made these features instant geologic celebrities by selling their images throughout the park.

From the Old Faithful Visitor Center, follow one or several of the trails and boardwalks that loop past the features of the Upper Geyser Basin. You will see nature's many and varied creations, including **Beehive, Castle, Grand, Giant, Riverside,** and **Daisy** geysers. Some geysers, like **Anemone,** perform perfectly and frequently, spouting water 10 feet (3 m) into the air every seven to ten minutes. Others are more sedate. **Grotto** spouts only about twice a day, but with powerful 20-minute eruptions up to 90 feet (27 m) high. Look also for the appropriately named hot springs: **Heart Spring, Beauty Pool,** and **Chromatic Spring.**

The **Grand Loop Road** heads southeast out of the Upper Geyser Basin toward **West Thumb** on **Yellowstone Lake.** After about 1.5 miles (2.4 km), look for **Kepler Cascades.** A wooden platform provides a wonderful view of this series of falls and cascades in the **Firehole River.** Tumbling 100 to 150 feet (30–45 m) between steep canyon walls, the cascades are now fully re-vealed. The same North Fork fire that swept through the **Madison Valley** in 1988 also cleared the greenery from this area.

Early park Superintendent P. W. Norris named Kepler Cascades in 1881 for a 12-year-old boy, Kepler Hoyt. Kepler had accompanied his father, Wyoming Governor John Hoyt, and a team of explorers in search of a prac-tical route between the park and Wyoming Territory. Norris noted that the "intrepid" youth "unflinchingly shared in all the hardships, privations and dangers of the explorations of his father."

A decade earlier, the cascades had captivated another adventurer, Lieu-tenant Gustavus C. Doane of the 1870 Washburn expedition, who wrote: "These pretty little falls if located on an eastern stream would be celebrated in history and song; here, amid objects so grand as to strain conception and stagger belief, they were passed without a halt."

Just south of Kepler Cascades, an old service road leads hikers, bikers, and skiers along the Firehole River to **Lone Star Geyser,** a round-trip dis-tance of 5 miles (8 km). The geyser's name apparently reflects its solitary status and has nothing to do with the Lone Star state of Texas. Water and steam jet 45 feet (13.5 m) into the air every three hours from Lone Star's steep-sided 12-foot (3.6 m) cone. An hour of minor water play precedes the 30-minute eruption. If you see Lone Star erupt, write the time and date on a slip of paper and attach it to the sign marking the area, then report your sighting at the Old Faithful Visitor Center. Your news will be much appreci-ated by those who follow.

Backpacking families can hike another 6 miles (9.6 km) over the Continental Divide to **Shoshone Geyser Basin** on the west shore of **Shoshone**

Examples of Geyser Activity in the Upper Basin *

Geyser	Average Interval Between Eruptions	Duration	Height
Old Faithful	76 min.	1.5–5.5 min.	105–184 ft. (32–56 m)
Beehive	14–27 hr.	4.5–5.25 min.	131–180 ft. (40–55 m)
Castle	11.5 hr.	15–20 min.	66–82 ft. (20–25 m)
Daisy	112 min.	3.5–4.5 min.	66–98 ft. (20–30 m)
Giant	3–4 days	90–115 min.	148–197 ft. (45–60 m)
Grand	9.5 hr.	9–16 min.	131–197 ft. (40–60 m)
Riverside	6.08 hr.	20 min.	66–82 ft. (20–25 m)

* Data on geyser eruptions from *1997 Ranger Naturalist Manual, Volume 1,*
Yellowstone National Park.

Yesterday's Morning Glory

At the close of the nineteenth century, engineer Hiram Chittenden described **Morning Glory Pool** as the epitome of tranquillity: "In this beautiful object the quiescent pool is at its best. Its exquisite bordering and the deep cerulean hue of its transparent waters make it, and others like it, objects of ceaseless admiration."

But admiration was not enough for many tourists. Bit by bit, Morning Glory's scalloped border was completely broken away by souvenir hunters. After an 1887 article in *Harper's New Monthly Magazine* eloquently described the pool's "long and slender throat, like the tube of the blossom, reaching from unknown depths below," its vent was choked off by coins and other objects tossed in by tourists. Morning Glory had become a wishing well. The Park Service eventually installed a padlocked box with a coin-drop beside the pool to receive the "good luck" offerings of superstitious visitors.

Reclamation efforts in 1950 retrieved more than a hundred different kinds of litter from Morning Glory's depths. In the 1970s, the **Grand Loop Road** was routed away from Morning Glory and the pool became a side trip at the end of the **Upper Geyser Basin** trail. Only then was it able to begin rebuilding its delicate sinter edging and reclaim some of its former beauty. The Park Service continues to clean Morning Glory periodically.

Damage caused by careless tourists endures. Constricted by debris still lodged deep in its throat, Morning Glory is much cooler than it once was. Bacteria grow in its crater. Despite its rehabilitation, Morning Glory will never again be as brilliant as it was a century ago.

The Pleasuring Ground

A summer visit to the **Upper Geyser Basin** is not complete without a stop at **Old Faithful Inn.** Stand in the center of the lobby, surrounded by the inn's gnarled staircases and balcony railings and its outsized timbered pillars and rafters, and listen to the stories they tell of presidents and royalty lounging in the overstuffed leather chairs, warming themselves by the fire. Five hundred tons (453.5 mt) of native stone were stacked and mortared to create the Brobdingnagian fireplace, which rises six stories to the roof and beyond. A gigantic clock of copper, wrought iron, and wood hangs from the massive chimney. Gulliver would recognize this place from his travels.

Honored as a National Historic Landmark, Old Faithful Inn was designed by Robert Reamer of Seattle, Washington, and built during the winter of 1903–1904. Its gabled east and west wings, also designed by Reamer, were added in 1913 and 1927.

While the architect captured the magic and whimsy of the thermal areas in his design for lodging, others capitalized on the unending source of hot water and, in 1924, built the world's largest geyser-water swimming pool on the hillside northeast of **Old Faithful.** The glass-roofed **Geyser Swimming Pool** was filled by the runoff from **Solitary Geyser:** 280,000 gallons (1,059,800 l) of naturally heated, constantly replenished water. The partitioned pool contained a 20-by-50-foot (6 x 15 m) area for children, a 50-by-150-foot (15 x 45 m) plunge for adults, and 147 dressing rooms. But a cement pool cannot last forever in an area of daily earth tremors. The pool closed in 1951, the building was razed in 1973, and the area was restored to its natural condition.

Facing the south side of **Old Faithful Geyser** is **Old Faithful Lodge,** remodeled in the 1930s from its raw beginnings as a tent camp for early motorists. The lodge provides dining and shopping opportunities to modern tourists.

Lake. The total round-trip distance from the Lone Star trailhead is 17 miles (27.2 km.) This is one of the few places in the park where you can still see a major geyser basin in a totally natural state. If you choose this hike, make sure you get a backcountry permit.

Remember to be extremely cautious when visiting remote thermal areas. The crust around geysers and hot springs is very thin and fragile. Careless visitors can be severely burned or even killed if they get too close to thermal features. Before venturing to Shoshone Geyser Basin or any other backcountry thermal area, contact a park ranger for a permit and more information.

Continuing east, the Grand Loop Road cuts through a pond that straddles the **Continental Divide** at **Craig Pass,** elevation 8,262 feet (2,510 m). From **Isa Lake,** water flows into both the Pacific and Atlantic oceans, but not the way you might think. During spring runoff, water draining from the western edge of the pond—which you would expect to go to the Pacific Ocean—flows west only as far as the Firehole and **Madison rivers,** and then it flows *east* into the Missouri, the Mississippi, the Gulf of Mexico, and the Atlantic Ocean. Water draining from the eastern edge—you would expect this to go to the Atlantic—actually flows east through several creeks and lakes to the **Lewis River,** then goes *west* via the Snake and Columbia rivers to the Pacific Ocean. During the rest of the year the pond drains to the west, its water eventually ending up in the Atlantic. Crazy? That's Isa Lake!

The Northern Pacific Railroad named this tiny lake in 1883 after a suggestion by Hiram Chittenden, the engineer who designed many of the park's early roads. Isa is short for Isabel Jelke, the first tourist to visit the lake. Chittenden wrote of the lake and Isabel: "Thou hast no name; pray, wilt though deign to bear/The name of her who first has sung of thee?"

Chittenden named Craig Pass in 1891, most likely in honor of the Craig family, especially Ida M. Craig Wilcox, "the first tourist to cross the pass" on his new road between Old Faithful and West Thumb.

Backcountry Adventure

No boardwalks, no cars, no crowds of tourists. Walk back in time to the days of mountain men like Jim Bridger and Osborne Russell, when this tract of backcountry was no more remote than anywhere else in the West.

Away from the **Grand Loop Road,** the **Shoshone Geyser Basin** has remained "off the beaten path," visited only by hikers, horseback riders, and canoeists. Here, the hearty trekker can see about 40 geysers within a 1,600-by-800-foot (480 x 240 m) area. Most were named by scientific survey teams in 1872 and 1878.

The geyser basin takes its name from **Shoshone Lake,** named in 1872 by the second Hayden survey party. Shoshone is the Indian name for the **Snake River,** which flows south from the park, and for the Indians themselves. The Shoshone or Snake people lived mostly to the west and south of Yellowstone, but they occasionally visited the area and may have come to this lake each summer. Their arrowheads and other artifacts have been found in various locations throughout the park.

Shoshone Lake is the second largest body of water in Yellowstone, with an area of 8,050 acres (3,260 ha) and a maximum depth of 205 feet (61.5 m). It is home to lake trout and brown trout, both planted in the late 1800s, and to Utah chubs, introduced without approval in the early 1900s.

You can also reach Shoshone Lake via a 6-mile (9.6 km) round-trip trail from **DeLacy Creek,** which is 8 miles (12.8 km) east of **Old Faithful.** The lake is an 8-mile (6.5 km) round-trip hike from **Dogshead Trailhead,** just north of **Lewis Lake** on the west side of the **South Entrance Road.** Or, go by water: the **Lewis Channel** is a canoe passage from Lewis Lake to Shoshone Lake.

Almost exactly midway between Old Faithful and West Thumb, the Grand Loop Road passes **Shoshone Point,** which offers a scenic view of Shoshone Lake. If the day is clear and sunny, you might also see the **Grand Tetons** even farther south.

A few miles later, the Grand Loop Road once again crosses the Continental Divide at 8,391 feet (2,558 m). A lodgepole pine forest lines both sides of the road. The density of this natural forest, and all forests throughout Yellowstone, reflects national park policy. Forests are never thinned; dead and fallen trees eventually decompose to become part of the soil, enriching it for future growth.

In a few more miles, you will see Yellowstone Lake. The **Absaroka Mountain Range** is on the lake's eastern edge.

South Entrance to West Thumb

22 miles (35 km)
Elevation at South Entrance: 6,886 feet (2,099 m)

✪ *The **South Entrance Road** is closed to motorized traffic from about the first Monday in November to the first Friday in May. **Summer facilities at Lewis Lake:** campground, boat ramp. **Winter facilities:** none. **Summer facilities at Grant Village:** visitor center, ranger station, amphitheater, campground, post office, lodging, food service, general store, service station, auto repair and towing, public showers, coin-operated laundry, boat ramp. **Winter facilities:** none.*

Driving north from **Grand Teton National Park,** you will be greeted by ghostly sentinels—dead-standing trees from the 1988 fires. Native bunchgrasses and young lodgepole pines have sprung up around the snags.

The **South Entrance Road** parallels the **Snake River** for a few miles. Mountain men named the river in 1812 for the Shoshone or Snake Indians. From its source on the **Two Ocean Plateau** in the southeast corner of the park, the Snake winds for 42 miles (68.2 km) through Yellowstone, then flows south to the **Grand Tetons,** coils north and south through the states of Idaho and Washington, and finally joins the Columbia River near Pasco, Washington. The Snake is the fifth longest river in the continental United States with a run of 1,038 miles (1,660.8 km).

Also south-flowing, the **Lewis River** feeds into the Snake about 1 mile (1.6 km) from the **South Entrance.** The South Entrance Road now follows this river upstream.

Almost immediately, the road begins a 2,000-foot (600 m) climb to the **Pitchstone Plateau,** on the southern boundary of the **Yellowstone Caldera.** Pitchstone is a type of rhyolite (solidified lava ash) found in rocks and soils throughout the park. The plateau was formed about 600,000 years ago, during one of Yellowstone's most recent volcanic eruptions.

At the edge of the Yellowstone Caldera, the river cuts through a deep canyon. A bridge spanning the canyon affords a good view of **Lewis Falls,** which drop 29 feet (9 m). The road and the river both flatten out as they pass through a narrow valley. This wetland is a good place to look for moose.

A little farther on, the highway follows the eastern shoreline of **Lewis Lake,** the third largest lake in the park. Lewis Lake is a great place to fish for brown trout. It also serves as a jumping-off point for backcountry hikers and canoeists. For a taste of the wild, take the **Lewis River Channel/Shoshone Lake Loop Trail.** The trailhead is just north of Lewis Lake on the west side of the road. The hike to the channel outlet at **Shoshone Lake** and back is 7 miles (11 km); it is 11 miles (17.5 km) if you return via the forested **Dogshead Trail.**

As you may have already guessed, Lewis River, Lewis Falls, and Lewis Lake were all named for Captain Meriwether Lewis of the Lewis and Clark Expedition.

After Lewis Lake, the road travels 6 miles (9.6 km) through a fire mosaic—a patchwork of burned and unburned areas created by the 1988 fires. In some places, healthy, mature trees stand next to a spot where every tree was torched. Areas cleared by fire now provide habitat for sun-loving grasses and forbs and the animals that need them for nourishment.

Finally, the South Entrance Road brings you to **Grant Village** on **Yellowstone Lake.** President Ulysses S. Grant, a controversial man in his own time, could not have foreseen the commotion surrounding the construction of the visitor center and commercial development bearing his name.

The Park Service conceived of Grant Village as a means to lessen congestion at **Old Faithful.** They also hoped the new tourist facility would relieve pressure on grizzly bears from developments at **West Thumb** and **Fishing Bridge,** where local spawning streams for native cutthroat trout attract a steady clientele of hungry grizzly and black bears between late May and early July. Human development interferes with the bears' survival. Ironically, just like the other two developments, Grant Village was built smack in the middle of prime grizzly bear habitat.

First planned in 1936, the Grant Village development was shelved more than half a dozen times. It finally came about piecemeal, starting with construction of the visitor center and ranger station in the late 1950s. Meanwhile, grizzly bear use of this area and others began to change. The garbage dumps were closed in the late 1960s and early 1970s, and the "no feeding" rule was enforced. The bears then turned to Fishing Bridge, where human fishing was now banned, and to spawning streams, which had previously gone unnoticed as significant to the growing trout population.

Along with the closure of all facilities at Fishing Bridge and the reversion of West Thumb to a day-use only area, Yellowstone's 1974 master plan promoted the development of Grant Village as a "wilderness threshold community" to encourage people to get out of their cars and into the backcountry. A 300-unit lodge and 425 campsites were built at Grant Village in the mid-1980s without adequate research on grizzly bear use of the area's five major spawning streams.

To date, the Park Service has removed a 320-site campground and all of the more than 300 wooden cabins at Fishing Bridge, and has rehabilitated the area. However, the 360-site AmFac RV park remains, and a visitor center, a general store, and an auto repair shop still provide services. Only an information station/bookstore, which doubles as a warming hut in winter, remains at West Thumb. To prevent clashes between bears and humans, the Park Service delays the opening of the Grant Village campground, also operated by AmFac Parks & Resorts, until the third week of June.

Interestingly, the Grant Village area is identified by Park Service ornithologist Terry McEneaney as "one of the best birding areas in the southern part of the Park." According to McEneaney, "a trip down to the lakefront could reward you with sightings of spotted sandpipers, ospreys, and even common mergansers."

West Thumb to Lake Junction

21 miles (34 km)
Elevation at West Thumb: 7,733 feet (2,357 m)

⊛ *Summer facilities at West Thumb Geyser Basin: information station/ bookstore. Winter facilities: warming hut, vending machines. Summer facilities at Bridge Bay: ranger station, amphitheater, campground, general store, marina, boat ramp. Winter facilities: none. Summer facilities at Lake Village: ranger station, hospital, post office, lodging, food service, general store. Winter facilities: none.*

The historic **West Thumb Ranger Station** serves as an information station and bookstore in the summer and becomes a cozy warming hut during the park's winter season. The ranger station was built in 1925, and the breezeway was added in 1966.

Look at the map. If you stretch your imagination, **Yellowstone Lake** looks a bit like a "human hand with the fingers extended and spread apart as much as possible," which is how members of the 1870 Washburn-Langford-Doane expedition described the lake. They called the lake's large west bay a thumb.

Notice that **West Thumb** is fairly round. It is actually the crater of a volcano, a newer and smaller one inside the huge **Yellowstone Caldera** that formed 600,000 years ago. A gigantic eruption some 150,000 years ago left this hole in the older caldera, making West Thumb deeper than most other parts of Yellowstone Lake. The maximum depth at West Thumb is 320 feet (96 m), while the lake's average depth is 139 feet (42 m).

Measuring about 4 by 6 miles (6.4 x 9.6 km), West Thumb is similar in size to Oregon's Crater Lake. A caldera created by a single volcano, Crater Lake is not a part of a more complex thermal region. The Crater Lake area is also a national park.

Feel the water here, and you may have trouble believing West Thumb is still one of Yellowstone's hot spots. About 2 yards (1.8 m) beneath the lake bottom, though, the mud is boiling. The magma from the volcano that created West Thumb is only 10,000 feet (3,000 m) farther down, and it creates some startling features along the lakeshore and under the water. In the summer, underwater geysers appear as slick spots or bulges on the lake's surface. In winter, round melt holes appear in the thick lake ice, as if someone has been ice fishing.

The offshore geysers along the narrow band of **West Thumb Geyser Basin** captured the fancy of mountain men and early park anglers. They caught trout in the cold mountain lake, then turned around and cooked them on-the-line in a boiling hot spring called **Fishing Cone.** Tourists would don cook hats and aprons to straddle the boiling hot spring, which resulted in a number of injuries. Fishing is no longer allowed here.

In late summer, you can see Fishing Cone and other lake thermal features from the 0.5-mile (0.8 km) boardwalk that loops through the geyser basin. Most features are submerged during the rest of the year. After a hiatus of 30 years, **Lakeshore Geyser** began erupting again on February 10, 2000, to a height of 10 feet (3 m). Since clearing its throat, Lakeshore continues to erupt to 2 to 3 feet (0.6–.09 m) about every 70 minutes. At one time, this offshore wonder shot water 50 feet (15 m) in the air.

Above the lake, West Thumb Geyser Basin contains many other interesting thermal features. With a depth of 53 feet (16 m), **Abyss Pool** is one of the deepest hot springs in the park. Its clear, hot water, ranging in color from a brilliant sapphire blue to emerald green, makes the pool look like a bottomless pit. In 1987, Abyss Pool became a geyser for a brief time; then, again during the winter of 1991–1992, it erupted several times a day, throwing water 30 to 80 feet (9–24 m) in the air. Since then it has been dormant.

Black Pool is actually blue now because it is so hot, but not too long ago it appeared black. Cooler temperatures allowed thick mats of brown and dark green bacteria to line its basin. Then, during the summer of 1991, Black Pool suddenly began to heat up. The heat killed the bacteria, and the pool finally erupted that August. It has only erupted a few times since. Black and Abyss pools show how dynamic this basin is.

The **West Thumb Paint Pots** were once compared to the beautiful **Fountain Paint Pots** in **Lower Geyser Basin,** but they became less active and less colorful in the early 1970s. The paint pots have shown renewed vigor in recent years, forming new mud cones and periodically throwing up mud.

The 3,100 gallons (11,733 l) of hot water that West Thumb Geyser Basin spills into Yellowstone Lake every day hardly affects the vast lake's average summer temperature of 45 degrees F (7°C). Swimming is *not* recommended in the West Thumb area or in any part of Yellowstone Lake. In late summer, the lake's water temperature varies according to its depth; the top layer of water rarely getting warmer than 66 degrees F (19°C). Lower layers are much, much colder. Survival time in such extremely cold water is only 20 to 30 minutes.

Watch for bison grazing around the geyser basin year-round, and for elk and mule deer in the summer and fall. From their high perches, bald eagles and ospreys scan the lake for trout. California gulls, green-winged teals, and common loons are often seen bobbing on the water. In winter, you may catch a glimpse of a river otter fishing for native cutthroat trout in open water or facing off with another animal that tried to steal its fish or scavenge its scraps.

From West Thumb, the **Grand Loop Road** takes you to **Bridge Bay** and **Lake Junction,** following the western shore of Yellowstone Lake, one of the largest mountain lakes in North America. Yellowstone Lake is nearly 1.5 miles (2.4 km) above sea level and about 20 miles (32 km) long and 14 miles (22.4 km) wide. The natural forces that formed the lake are the same ones that created other features in the park. The most recent volcanic explosions, 600,000 years ago, came from two vents: the **Mallard Lake Dome** near **Old Faithful,** and the **Sour Creek Dome** just north of **Fishing Bridge.** About two-thirds of Yellowstone Lake lies within the eastern portion of the caldera that formed when the magma chamber collapsed. The domes continue to bulge and subside an average of 1 inch (2.5 cm) each year.

The glaciers, springs, and seasonal runoff of the **Absaroka Mountain Range** to the east, as well as runoff from **Pitchstone Plateau** to the south and **Two Ocean Plateau** to the southeast, provide nearly all of Yellowstone Lake's water. Poised on the edge of the Continental Divide, the lake water sustains life in the **Greater Yellowstone Ecosystem** and beyond. Most of the water is

The Glittering Inland Sea

Nestled among the forest-crowned hills which bounded our vision, lay this inland sea, its crystal waves dancing and sparkling in the sunlight as if laughing with joy for their wild freedom. It is a scene of transcendent beauty which has been viewed by but few white men, and we felt glad to have looked upon it before its primeval solitude should be broken by the crowds of pleasure seekers which at no distant day will throng its shores.

—David Folsom,
1869

Folsom's words capture the essence of **Yellowstone Lake.** Because roads trace less than half its 110 miles (176 km) of shoreline, most of this glittering body of water and its attendant riparian areas still enjoy "primeval solitude," providing refuge for birds and mammals. The Park Service keeps the western part of **Flat Mountain Arm** and the southern portions of the **South and Southeast arms** (or fingers, if you continue to view the lake as a hand) closed to motorized craft to protect critical wildlife habitat like the **Molly Islands.** Tucked deep into the Southeast Arm, the Molly Islands provide sanctuary to the American white pelicans that nest and breed there. The islands were named for Molly Gannett, the wife of Henry Gannett, an astronomer and topographer for the second Hayden survey in 1878.

channeled through the **Yellowstone River,** which is also one of the lake's preeminent feeder streams. Since the lake basin has a capacity of 12.1 million acre-feet of water and its annual outflow is about 1.1 million acre-feet, scientists estimate that the lake's water is completely replaced only about every 10 to 12 years. Since 1952, the depth of Yellowstone Lake has fluctuated less than 6 feet (1.8 m) a year.

Stop at any of the picnic areas along the lake and watch for American white pelicans. They work cooperatively to force fish into shallow water, where the birds can scoop them up in their big bills. Contrary to popular belief, pelicans don't dive; they swim just below the surface of the water or they wade. They don't stow schools of fish in their large bill pouches, either. Each time a pelican catches a fish, it drains the water from its pouch, throws its head back, and swallows the fish whole.

You will see plenty of California gulls here, too. Notice the red mark on the lower bill of the adult gulls. Baby gulls peck at this target to tell their parents they are hungry.

More than likely, the pelicans and gulls—and other birds as well—are catching native cutthroat trout. Yellowstone Lake has the largest native cutthroat trout population in the world.

Just before Bridge Bay, the Grand Loop Road passes a hook of land called **Gull Point,** a nice place for a picnic with an expansive view of the lake. Here, you are in a spruce and Douglas-fir forest. Look for songbirds: brown creepers, golden-crowned kinglets, ruby-crowned kinglets, mountain chickadees, red-breasted nuthatches, Swainson's thrushes, and hermit thrushes.

Try your luck on Yellowstone Lake! MIKE SAMPLE PHOTO

Natives and Nonnatives

About 8,000 years ago, native cutthroat trout, and perhaps longnose dace, made their way to **Yellowstone Lake** after swimming up the **Snake River** to its headwaters at **Two Ocean Pass,** south of the park boundary. Two Ocean Pass is similar to **Isa Lake** in that its waters travel to both the Atlantic and Pacific oceans. Two streams flow through a meadow at Two Ocean Pass: one is clogged by beaver dams, and the other splits, each branch following its own course to either the Atlantic or Pacific.

Native cutthroat trout naturally thrive in the clean, open water of Yellowstone Lake. They do so well that between 1900 and 1955, more than 800 million eggs were "farmed" in a fish hatchery and distributed to fisheries throughout the world. Meanwhile, exotic species were introduced to the lake system, including longnose suckers, redside shiners, and lake chub.

During that same period, commercial and sport fishing removed a total of 48 million mature trout from the lake. Many of these fish were taken at the lake's **Yellowstone River** outlet at **Fishing Bridge.** In the 1960s, the native cutthroat trout population collapsed. At first, managers limited lake anglers to 20 native cutthroat trout per day. They set progressively more restrictive limits until they finally banned fishing altogether on Fishing Bridge. Over the next 20 years, the fishery made a remarkable comeback.

Then real trouble began. In 1994, a young visitor caught a lake trout in Yellowstone Lake. It was as if a fire alarm went off, and the ringing has not ceased. Lake trout, or Mackinaws, are not native to Yellowstone Lake and somehow they had been illegally introduced. Their very presence could sound a death knell for the lake's native cutthroat trout.

Native cutthroat trout thrive at or near the surface of Yellowstone Lake, returning each year to nearby streams and rivers to spawn (lay their eggs). They eat insects and freshwater shrimp, and they are food for grizzly bears, ospreys, bald eagles, and other wildlife.

Lake trout, on the other hand, prey on other fish. They live out most of their lives in cold, deep water, visiting shallower lake waters each fall to lay their eggs and feast on native cutthroat trout and other species. They have no predators among the wildlife of Yellowstone.

When lake trout have been introduced elsewhere, they have made short work of native fish populations. In no time at all, the native fish disappeared, consumed by the larger and more aggressive lake trout. Without constant vigilance and management techniques, lake trout could wipe out Yellowstone Lake's population of native cutthroat trout and upset the life cycle of countless other species, including the threatened grizzly bear. After the first lake trout was caught, the Park Service immediately began gill-netting these fish intruders and requiring anglers to keep all lake trout they catch. Anglers can help further by taking lake trout to a ranger station for examination.

Now that lake trout have entered Yellowstone Lake, it is impossible to eradicate them, but aggressive management may keep them from overwhelming native species and upsetting the delicate natural balance of the Yellowstone ecosystem.

Bridge Bay, a boater's haven, isn't far down the road. Yellowstone Lake has a long and colorful history of boating. Though Native Americans and fur trappers probably floated rafts on the lake much earlier, the *Anna,* launched in 1871 by the Hayden survey party, was the first recorded craft on the lake. In the summer of 1889, the first sightseeing steamboat, operated by E. C. Waters and his Yellowstone Lake Boat Company, plied the lake's waters more. The *Zillah* was 81 feet (24.3 m) long and 14 feet (4.2 m) at the beam. She could tote 120 passengers from the stagecoach lunch station at West Thumb Bay to **Lake Yellowstone Hotel,** with an intermediate stop on **Dot Island** to see the penned bison and elk Waters kept there. Today, **Bridge Bay Marina** is filled with boats.

The hazards created by Yellowstone Lake's sheer size and depth are the same as they were for the lake's earliest pioneers. Strong prevailing winds can sometimes whip the lake into a tempestuous inland ocean. Capsizing in cold water can kill boaters within minutes. Extreme caution is advised.

Freeze-up on the lake can begin as early as December, producing ice up to 3 feet (0.9 m) thick by Christmas Day. The process gradually turns the lake into a 136-square-mile (354 k^2) ice cube, frozen solid from shore to shore except for thermal melt holes. Snow covers the ice for a good six months. Break-up, in late May or early June, happens quickly.

Yellowstone Lake is a magical place in the winter, with its broad ice field and a vista of snowy mountains punctuated by puffs of steam from thermal features. But it is most accessible in the summertime. Make the most of it!

Take a flat, meandering trail near the entrance to the **Bridge Bay Campground** to explore **Natural Bridge,** one of Yellowstone's many natural wonders. This cool, easy walk through the forest leads to the capstone of a 51-foot-high (18 m) cliff of rhyolite rock that was eroded away by **Bridge Creek.** F. V. Hayden discovered this bit of natural engineering in 1871, but at the time, named only the creek. The more descriptive "Natural Bridge" eventually became the formation's official name. You can get to Natural Bridge via a 2-mile (3.2 km) path that starts just south of AmFac's Bridge Bay Campground, or, take the 3-mile-loop (5 km) bike trail, which traces an old wagon route, starting just south of the marina on the Grand Loop Road. Look for yellow-rumped warblers as you hike or bike. Both trails, as well as Bridge Bay Campground, are closed from late spring to early summer while bears feast on the trout spawning in Bridge Creek.

A couple of miles from Bridge Bay, the Grand Loop Road brings you to **Lake Village.** Built by the Northern Pacific Railroad, the yellow and white clapboard Lake Yellowstone Hotel opened in 1891 on a knoll above the lake long known as a rendezvous site for Indians and mountain men. In 1903, Robert Reamer, architect of the **Old Faithful Inn,** supervised the addition of ionic columns, 15 false balconies, and other renovations. The dining room, portico, and sunroom were added in 1929. A ten-year restoration project led to the hotel's centennial celebration and its 1991 inclusion on the National Register of Historic Places.

Robert Reamer designed **Lake Lodge** in 1926 to fill a more relaxed niche by providing rustic cabins and a main lodge for dining and other visitor services. Lake Lodge does not open until mid-June, and the cabins nearest **Lodge Creek** remain closed until after spawning season.

Another historic building still in use is **Lake Ranger Station**. Stephen Mather, the first director of the National Park Service, suggested the building be designed to blend in with its natural and cultural environment. Yellowstone Superintendent Horace M. Albright heeded his boss's wishes and hired a local woodsman to build a trapper-style cabin. The ranger station includes a large octagonal hall with a central stone fireplace, perfect for gatherings on chilly evenings. It was completed in 1923.

A few miles beyond Lake Village, the **East Entrance Road** joins the Grand Loop Road.

East Entrance to Lake Junction

27 miles (43 km)
Elevation at East Entrance: 6,951 feet (2,119 m)

⭐ *The **East Entrance Road** is closed from about the first Monday in November to the first Friday in May. **Summer facilities at Fishing Bridge:** museum, visitor center, RV campground, general store, service station, auto repair, public showers, coin-operated laundry. **Winter facilities:** warming hut, vending machines, snowmobile fuel.*

After traveling the 53 miles (85 km) from the gateway community of **Cody, Wyoming,** be prepared for traffic delays as you enter the park: a ten-year reconstruction project began in 1994 on the **East Entrance Road.** Fortunately, subalpine scenic grandeur will ease your wait in the construction zone. As the route's designer said long ago, "This road is throughout its length one of exceptional scenic attraction, and will always be of great interest to travelers."

Like the **Northeast Entrance Road,** the road from the East Entrance cuts through the **Absaroka Mountain Range.** You will quickly ascend to the 8,530-foot (2,600 m) **Sylvan Pass,** the site of frequent winter avalanches. The pass must take its name from the lake below because, as noted in an early road guide, "there is nothing of a sylvan character in the pass itself." Indeed, the pass looks like a giant trench through a rock pile.

West of the pass, the road gently descends to **Eleanor Lake,** which is about 6 miles (9.6 km) from the park entrance. Hiram Chittenden, who worked on the park's road system between 1891 and 1893, named the lake for his infant daughter. You will soon reach lovely, wooded **Sylvan Lake,** where you may see striking black and white (male) ducks called Barrow's goldeneyes. Both Eleanor and Sylvan lakes were carved out by glaciers that crept over the Absaroka Mountains 200,000 years ago.

Beyond the lakes, the East Entrance Road sweeps down the mountains to **Yellowstone Lake.** Take the 1-mile (1.6 km) side road north to **Lake Butte** overlook. On a clear day, you can see the entire lake basin, including the **Washburn Range** to the northwest, **Central Plateau** directly across the lake to the west, and **Two Ocean Plateau** to the south, where streams flow to both the Atlantic and Pacific oceans. The **Grand Teton Mountain Range** is 60 miles (96 km) to the southwest. Closer at hand, you may see blue grouse and Clark's nutcrackers.

The road now follows the shoreline of Yellowstone Lake. Between Lake Butte and **Steamboat Point,** it curls around **Sedge Bay,** where researchers recently discovered underwater thermal activity. The lakeside fumaroles and hot springs of **Steamboat Springs** remind us of the forces that continue to affect the landscape of Yellowstone. You are now on the eastern edge of the great **Yellowstone Caldera.** Watch for ospreys, California gulls, American white pelicans, trumpeter swans, and ducks of many species.

Next, the road parallels another rounded cut-out on the shoreline, a neat little bay christened by early tourists in 1873 to honor one of their party, Mary Clark, "a young lady from Chicago, with vocal gifts that all admired." **Mary Bay** was formed by a steam explosion long ago. Today it is the hottest spot in Yellowstone Lake.

Between Mary Bay and the East Entrance Road lies an inland pond formed by another steam explosion. In 1880, Park Superintendent P. W. Norris named this small body of water **Indian Pond,** since it had been a favorite campsite for Native Americans.

Park at the pullout and follow the 3-mile (4.8 km) **Storm Point Trail** that leads around Indian Pond and along the shore of Yellowstone Lake. From the open meadows between Indian Pond and Yellowstone Lake, the path takes a sharp right (west) turn through the lodgepole pine forest along the lakeshore, and

Yellowstone National Park, 390 Feet (117 m) Below

If you could empty **Yellowstone Lake,** you would find geysers, hot springs, fumaroles, waterfalls, and deep canyons—all the features you have been exploring, but much, much farther down! Recent research by Val Klump of the Great Lakes Institute and the University of Wisconsin exposed this new frontier and revamped our knowledge about Yellowstone Lake.

Before Klump's research, scientists assumed that at 320 feet (96 m) deep, **West Thumb's** floor was the deepest and hottest spot in the lake. This turned out to be wrong. A small robotic submarine probing the lake under Klump's direction found a canyon 390 feet (117 m) deep just east of **Stevenson Island.** Klump found underwater thermal features at West Thumb, of course, and at **Mary and Sedge bays,** but Mary Bay's hot bottom, at 252 degrees F (122°C), took the prize for the hottest spot in the lake. The submarine found some curious piping for dormant underwater geysers in Mary Bay, as well.

The robot also showed researchers that the floor of Yellowstone Lake is similar to a ridge thousands of feet lower in the middle of the Pacific Ocean. There, the nutrient- and mineral-rich cones of hydrothermal vents support an abundance of plant and animal life, including bacterial mats, sponges, and earthworms.

continues through the trees to scenic and windswept **Storm Point.** The rocky area near the point is home to a large colony of yellow-bellied marmots. The trail follows the shoreline and eventually loops back through the forest to Indian Pond. Sometimes the trail is closed because of grizzly bear activity; stop at a ranger station or visitor center to find out.

Throughout the ages, Indian Pond was a convenient place for Native Americans to manufacture implements and hunt game near the quarries and lush wildlife habitat of **Pelican Valley.** As many as 9,600 years ago, Native Americans summered along the shores of Yellowstone Lake. They left evidence of their passage in the many projectile points, hearths, and other artifacts that have since been found in the area.

Two miles (3.2 km) west of Indian Pond, the East Entrance Road crosses **Pelican Creek.** The creek and valley were named in 1864 when a prospector mistakenly shot a pelican, thinking it was a goose. An-

The Nez Perce in Yellowstone

In 1877, five nontreaty bands of Nez Perce Indians camped overnight by **Indian Pond** while fleeing the U.S. Army, trying to avoid forced relocation to a government reservation. Imagine the scene as nearly 700 people set up camp, bringing 1,500 horses to the pond to drink. The following day, the Nez Perce set out on the last leg of their sad journey. They traveled across the **Absaroka Mountains** to seek sanctuary with the Crow Nation, only to learn that the Crow had befriended the Army. The nontreaty bands turned north and headed for Canada and freedom. After a journey of 1,700 miles (2,720 km), the Nez Perce were captured in the **Bear's Paw Mountains** of Montana, just 40 miles (64 km) from the Canadian border.

other short, easy trail that explores a variety of habitats starts from the west end of the bridge. **Pelican Creek Trail** loops 1 mile (1.6 km) through the forest to the shore of Yellowstone Lake. It leads across a marsh where you might see moose, especially in the early morning or evening. Watch for the birds that rely on this riparian habitat: green-winged teals, ospreys, and American white pelicans.

Pelican Valley, which lies to the north of the Pelican Creek bridge, and **Hayden Valley** to the northwest provide some of the best habitat for grizzly bears, bison, elk, and other wildlife in the continental United States. For that reason, overnight camping is not permitted in either place and seasonal restrictions further limit human activity to avoid conflicts with wildlife.

One mile (1.6 km) beyond Pelican Creek, the East Entrance Road crosses the **Yellowstone River** at **Fishing Bridge.** The development complex at Fishing Bridge has caused problems for bears, but human visitor use was

Gentle Storm Point Trail traverses a grassy meadow by Indian Pond, then cuts through the forest to the rocky shoreline of Yellowstone Lake. MIKE SNYDER PHOTO

established in the early years of the park and has become a habit that is nearly impossible to break. In those first days, tourists camped along the banks of the Yellowstone River and pulled in big catches of native cutthroat trout that came to spawn (lay their eggs) at the outflow of Yellowstone Lake.

The first bridge over the river, fashioned of rough-hewn logs in 1902, set the stage for further development. Tent camps and other concessions soon followed. In 1931, the park added the **Fishing Bridge Museum and Visitor Center** to help tourists learn about the park's diverse flora and fauna. The building's rustic architecture, featuring native timbers and rock pillars, earned the museum recognition as a National Historic Landmark.

The present peeled-log bridge, bigger and better than the first, was built in 1937 to accommodate automobiles and subsequent increases in traffic. The 1950s brought more tourist facilities to the area, and anglers elbowed for casting room along the pedestrian lanes lining both sides of this newer bridge.

All this pressure on the fishery contributed to a decline in the native cutthroat trout population and an increase in conflicts between humans and bears. Short of fish, the bears sometimes turned to the tourists' groceries or garbage as alternative food sources. In 1973, the Park Service closed Fishing Bridge to human fishing; in 1989, the park banned tent camping in the area. Fishing Bridge continues to be an excellent place to watch fish.

Not far beyond Fishing Bridge, the East Entrance Road meets the **Grand Loop Road.**

Lake Junction to Canyon Junction

16 miles (26 km)
Elevation at Lake Junction: 7,784 feet (2,373 m)

⚙ *Summer facilities at Lake Village: ranger station, hospital, post office, lodging, food service, general store.* **Winter facilities:** *none.*

About 3 miles (4.8 km) north of **Fishing Bridge,** the **Grand Loop Road** brings you to **LeHardy Rapids.** From here the **Yellowstone River** rushes over a boulder-strewn streambed.

If you visit LeHardy Rapids in June or July, the river will be crammed from bank to bank with native cutthroat trout swimming upstream to spawn near Fishing Bridge. Take the short trail along the river and watch the action! You may see fish resting in pools at the edge of the river. They are gathering energy to make Herculean leaps up the rapids or preparing for an underwater assault against the strong current. Instincts draw these fish back to their birthplace to lay their eggs.

The rapids were named for Paul LeHardy, a civilian cartographer who joined the W. A. Jones military reconnaissance of Wyoming and Yellowstone National Park in 1873. This turbulent stretch is probably where LeHardy and a companion lost their raft and other gear while attempting to sketch the river and measure its depth.

The Grand Loop Road now follows the Yellowstone River north through the **Yellowstone Caldera.** The longest free-flowing stream in the lower 48 states, the Yellowstone River begins high in the snowfields of the **Absaroka Mountains** southeast of the park. It feeds **Yellowstone Lake,** then runs its course for 671 miles (1,074 km) before joining the Missouri River in North Dakota.

Six miles (9.6 km) from **Lake Junction,** you can take a 0.7-mile (1 km) footpath through the **Mud Volcano** area. Here, caldrons of hissing and spitting mud bubble furiously, bringing to mind witches and their monstrous brews. Steam from the hot springs has hard-boiled the trees in this bleak landscape. And the smell! Hydrogen sulfide gas, the same gas that forms inside rotting eggs, will take your breath away. The highly acidic water makes a plastic stew of volcanic clays, which burp and collapse in all sorts of weird configurations, releasing the gas you smell.

When the Washburn-Langford-Doane expedition discovered the Mud Volcano itself in 1870, it was 30 feet (9 m) in diameter and it exploded regularly with a sound "resembling discharges of gun-boat mortar." Mud spattered nearby trees as high as 200 feet (60 m) up their trunks and steam rose 300 feet (90 m) in the air—more than twice the height of **Old Faithful.**

In 1872 Nathaniel Langford, Washburn expedition member and now the park's first superintendent, returned to Mud Volcano to see what he and the others had thought was one of Yellowstone's most remarkable features. Langford was sorely disappointed. In the two years since his first visit, the Mud Volcano had blown out its plumbing. Since then, the volcano and the surrounding area have constantly changed. Much of the steamy earth now looks like a quarry or an excavation site.

The footpath leads you past the area's thermal features, many of which have colorful recent histories. When it burst onto the scene in 1948, **Black Dragon's Caldron** ripped up trees by their roots and plastered the area with mud. In 1978–1979, a succession of small, shallow earthquakes turned up the heat and created **Cooking Hillside.** High temperatures baked the grasses and trees that covered this slope—and remained boiling hot.

Look for **Dragon's Mouth Spring**, so named because it used to belch steam and snake out a tongue of water. Then, in December 1994, Dragon's Mouth was suddenly calm—at least outwardly. You can still hear the subterranean crash of its hot water against unseen cavern walls. About the time Dragon's Mouth "tamed down," **Mud Geyser** began stirring to life. In 1993, soil temperatures around Mud Geyser soared, and in January 1995, the geyser began rocketing steam skyward, blanching the surrounding hillside. Take

Catch a whiff of the potent Mud Volcano. WILLIAM NICHOLS PHOTO

a look at some of the other features here, too, like **Sizzling Basin, Churning Caldron, Sour Lake,** and **Grizzly Fumarole.**

Just across the Grand Loop Road is the yellow **Sulphur Caldron,** one of Yellowstone's most acidic hot springs. With a pH of about 1.2, Sulphur Caldron is as sour as stomach fluids or the acid inside your car battery. This potent hot spring is eating away part of the parking area. The yellow color comes from all the sulfur (rotten eggs again!) in the spring.

The Mud Volcano and Sulphur Caldron thermal areas are on the southern edge of the broad, fairly flat **Hayden Valley.** The valley bears the name of Dr. Ferdinand Hayden, who explored Yellowstone for the U.S. Geological Survey. Hayden's first expedition, in 1871, came back with scientific information as well as photographs and paintings of the area. These first images of Yellowstone helped convince Congress the region was indeed a special place that should be preserved. Over a period of several years, Hayden mapped **Lower Geyser Basin,** found a route between the basin and Yellowstone Lake, and surveyed the lake's shoreline.

Long ago, a glacier dammed the 50-square-mile (129.5 km²) Hayden Valley and filled it with water. The valley became an arm of Yellowstone Lake. When the water receded, a thick layer of glacial till (a mix of clay, sand, and gravel) covered the valley floor, overlaying the fine-grained lake sediments. The clay and sediments form an impermeable layer that cannot support tree growth, but they do provide rich habitat for shrubs and grasses. The valley's rolling meadows are an important winter range for bison and

Hayden Valley offers some of the best wildlife viewing in the park. MIKE SAMPLE PHOTO

elk, and a year-round haven for bison, elk, deer, moose, and predators such as grizzly bears and coyotes.

Where the Yellowstone River meanders through the Hayden Valley, glacial kettles catch water and form marshes. Tall grasses and reeds grow, sheltering moose and migratory waterfowl all along the valley.

Hayden Valley is a natural sanctuary. Watch for trumpeter swans floating serenely on the quiet water and great blue herons wading in the shallows on their long stilt-like legs, searching for fish, toads, and insects. Look for regal Canada geese, with their black heads and necks, white chin straps, and grayish brown bodies, and for mallard ducks feeding in the shallow water, tails up. Other ducks—Barrow's goldeneyes and mergansers—dive head first into the river for fish. Ospreys plummet feet-first into the water after fish, and they rarely miss.

Our national bird, the bald eagle (its white head is not really bald), nests in the pines away from the river. You may also see marsh hawks gliding a few feet above the grasslands and marshes as they search for rodents.

This stretch of the Yellowstone River is one of the finest fishing streams in the park. More than 30 years ago the only "wildlife" in Hayden Valley were anglers who literally lined the banks of the Yellowstone River. The anglers drove the real wildlife away. In 1965, the Park Service finally banned human fishing in Hayden Valley. After a time, the waterfowl, moose, and other animals returned. This stretch of the river continues to be a fine fishing stream for the animals that depend on it, and now the valley is one of the best places in the park to see wildlife.

Hayden Valley is also one of the best places in Yellowstone to see grizzly bears, especially in the spring and early summer when they prey on newborn bison and elk calves. You might see large herds of bison here any time, but you are almost sure to see them in the spring and early summer and during the rut (mating season) in late July and August.

At the northern edge of Hayden Valley, the Grand Loop Road crosses **Alum Creek.** Mountain man Jim Bridger claimed that the creek's warm, mineralized water would shrink a horse's hooves.

Just beyond Alum Creek, the valley narrows and suddenly becomes a great chasm—the **Grand Canyon of the Yellowstone River.** Cross the elegant arch of the **Chittenden Bridge**, park, and follow the **South Rim Trail** a short distance to view **Upper Falls.** Here, the Yellowstone River tumbles 109 feet (33 m) to the canyon floor. It is hard to believe this is the same river that wandered so peacefully through the Hayden Valley just a moment ago. The water leaps over the falls with a thunderous roar, ever cutting away more rock and soil from the canyon walls.

The partially paved South Rim Trail continues 3.25 miles (5.2 km) farther to **Point Sublime.** The canyon area has several other trails of varying

The Grand Canyon
of the Yellowstone River

As you look at the falls of the **Yellowstone River,** you might wonder how such a deep canyon could be gouged out of hard rock. The simple answer is that though some of the rock is hard, some of it is soft and easily eroded by rushing water. But the "why" of the canyon takes a little more explaining.

Surprisingly, not a lot is known about how the **Grand Canyon of the Yellowstone River** was formed. What's more, Park Service geologists doubt the validity of the little field work that has been done here. They will say, however, that erosion, not glaciation, did the work.

Geologists believe the doming action before the **Yellowstone Caldera** erupted 600,000 years ago caused a fault at the site of the present canyon. After the eruption, lava oozing from the caldera overran the canyon area. The extensive faulting, the lava, and subsurface heat (related to the doming and faulting) created a thermal area that you can still see today. Look for puffs of steam escaping below **Lower Falls.**

Glaciers filled the canyon at least twice, creating ice dams along the Yellowstone River and at the mouth of **Yellowstone Lake.** About 14,000 years ago, when the dams melted, a huge rush of water caused catastrophic erosion and carved the canyon as we know it today. A lot of soft, thermally altered rock washed downstream, while harder, unaltered rock at the brinks of the waterfalls did not erode as easily.

Water, wind, earthquakes, and other natural forces continue to erode and sculpt the canyon. Today, the canyon's depth varies from 800 to 1,200 feet (240–360 m); at its narrowest and widest points the canyon is 1,500 and 4,000 feet (450 m and 1,200 m) wide; and it is 20 miles (32 km) long, from **Upper Falls** to the **Tower Fall** area. This deep gorge was a barrier to early explorers. Still, they recognized the Grand Canyon of the Yellowstone River, along with the geyser basins and Yellowstone Lake, as a place worth preserving for all time.

lengths and difficulty. Talk to a ranger or ask for a trail guide at the **Canyon Visitor Center.** Remember, all of the trails could be wet and slippery and many are steep. Wear comfortable, sturdy shoes, carry water, and hike with caution. Many trails are closed in the late fall, winter, and early spring because of ice.

Stop at the Upper Falls parking area on **South Rim Drive** for a spectacular view of the **Brink of the Upper Falls.** If you want to watch the water rush over the precipice, and don't mind stairs, take the 0.25-mile (0.4 km) trail.

From the Upper Falls parking area, you can take the South Rim Trail to see **Crystal Falls** (between Upper and Lower falls), where **Cascade Creek** plunges into the canyon below. A platform offers you a picture-perfect look at this sheet of water plummeting 129 feet (38.7 m) to the Yellowstone River.

The Washburn-Langford-Doane exploration party gave Crystal Falls and Cascade Creek their names. P. W. Norris, the park's second superintendent, was truly captivated by the falls. His poem "Rustic Bridge and Crystal Falls" eulogizes the falls and a cavelike pool just above the brink.

> Skipping rill from snowy fountains
> Dashing through embow'red walls,
> Fairy dell 'mid frowning mountains,
> Grotto pool and Crystal falls.
>
> Here we part perchance forever,
> In our pilgrimage below;
> Yet in scenes like these together,
> Above may we each other know.

Uncle Tom's Trail also starts from the Upper Falls parking lot on the **South Rim,** and leads to a view of the base of Lower Falls and of the canyon itself.

Back at the top of the canyon, continue along the South Rim Trail or South Rim Drive to **Artist Point.** Can you tell how Artist Point got its name? The view encompasses the many colors in the canyon walls. The rock at the top of the canyon is nearly black; other rocks are gray, light pink, or lavender. Still other layers have been stained shades of orange and yellow. During his

Use caution at viewing points for the magnificent Grand Canyon of the Yellowstone River.
Mike Sample photo

tour of the area with the 1871 Hayden survey, artist Thomas Moran adroitly captured the image and the mood of the Grand Canyon of the Yellowstone River, but he said "its beautiful tints were beyond the reach of human art."

Notice the rock that looks like lightweight concrete with bits of rock embedded in it. This is welded tuff, formed when molten rock burst from a long-ago volcano, then stuck together and hardened as it cooled.

Look for the high brushpile nests of ospreys or fish hawks as you pause at Artist Point. (You may also see the nests from **Grandview** and **Lookout points** on the **North Rim**.) Like eagles, ospreys mate for life and return to the same nest each year, from late April until late August or early September.

Uncle Tom's Trail

Tom Richardson built the first trail into the **Grand Canyon of the Yellowstone River** in 1898 to offer a special experience to early Yellowstone tourists. Uncle Tom picked up his customers at their hotel across the canyon (where the horse corrals are now located), about 1 mile (1.6 km) south of **Canyon Junction.** He ferried them across the **Yellowstone River** above **Upper Falls**. After disembarking, the tourists walked along the canyon rim to a point below **Lower Falls** and climbed down 528 rungs on rope ladders. At the bottom of the canyon, they revelled in the spray of Lower Falls, ate dinner, then climbed back up the ladders and ferried the river to their hotel. All this for fifty cents a person.

Around the turn of the century, tourists always traveled in their best clothes. Imagine the men in their suits and the women in their long, full woolen skirts, sodden with the spray of the falls, hoisting themselves back up the ladder and hiking that trail! Uncle Tom Richardson lost his business permit in 1903 when **Chittenden Bridge** was completed.

Later, a second **Uncle Tom's Trail** was built: a series of wood and stone steps connected by trails led to a platform on a knob between the present landing and the river. This trail closed in the early 1960s when it was deemed unsafe. The present trail opened in the mid-1990s. It is a combination of bridges, concrete steps, pavement, and, finally, more than 300 metal steps leading to a platform about 500 feet (150 m) below the **South Rim** of the canyon.

The view from the platform is awesome. The water leaps from the brink of Lower Falls and crashes to the river 308 feet (94 m) below, twice the plunge of New York's famed Niagara Falls. Notice how much cooler it is on the platform, and feel the force of the water as it thunders into the pool below. Look for the rainbow in the mist that shrouds the bottom third of the falls. Wave at the ant-sized people above you, at the **Brink of the Lower Falls** on the **North Rim.**

A gouge in the lip of Lower Falls causes the green stripe you see; the water that passes over the gouged part doesn't get frothy dropping over the edge. The green is the result of the depth of the water in the gouge, the angle of your view, and the amount of light hitting the falls at that point.

Catch some inspiring views at Inspiration Point. MIKE SAMPLE PHOTO

Continue up the Grand Loop Road to **Canyon Village** and turn east at the intersection onto the one-way **North Rim Drive.** In about 1 mile (1.6 km), follow the left fork for 1 mile (1.6 km) to **Inspiration Point.** Along the way, you can see a great example of the power of glaciers. A huge granite boulder, 24 by 20 by 18 feet (7.2 x 6 x 5.4 m), sits right in the middle of the tree-covered landscape. This 500-ton (453.5 mt) glacial boulder was pushed or carried by a glacier tens of thousands of years ago. The nearest granite outcropping is in the northeast corner of the park, so the boulder traveled at least 20 miles (32 m).

The only way to get to the very bottom of the canyon is to hike the strenuous **Seven Mile Hole Trail,** an all-day 11-mile (18 km) round-trip prospect. This hike is not for slouches. It starts at the **Glacial Boulder Trailhead** on the North Rim, deceiving you for an easy 2 miles (3.2 km) along the canyon rim. One mile (1.6 km) after the Seven Mile Hole Trail joins the **Washburn Spur Trail,** it plummets to **Seven Mile Hole:** you'll go 1,400 feet (420 m) down in 1.5 miles (2.4 km). The descent takes you past hot springs; some are dormant, some are not, so be careful. Dipping water ouzels and soaring ospreys might provide a show when you reach the river's edge. Save some energy for the long hike back up the trail.

At the end of the road to Inspiration Point is a parking area. From here, more than 50 steps lead down to the point itself, which offers a view up the canyon to Lower Falls and beyond. The river winds through the canyon about 900 feet (270 m) below.

Other trails along North Rim Drive also lead to spectacular views. From Lookout Point, you may see violet-green swallows darting in and out of their "condominiums" along the canyon walls. The birds take advantage of cracks and crevices to build their cuplike nests. Swallows are strong and elegant in flight, catching flying insects in midair.

If you stop at the southernmost parking lot on North Rim Drive, you can take a steep trail 0.75 mile (1.2 km) to the **Brink of the Lower Falls.** The trail drops about 600 feet (180 m) in that short distance, so do not attempt it if you have health problems. If you do brave the trail, you can get "up close and personal" to the power of water in a hurry. During spring runoff, usually in June, 63,500 gallons (240,348 l) of water pass over this rim every second. By November, a mere 5,000 gallons (18,925 l) per second rush over the perpendicular drop. Look across the canyon to the base of **Uncle Tom's Trail** and wave back at the people waving at you.

Canyon Junction to Norris Junction

12 miles (19 km)
Elevation at Canyon Junction: 7,734 feet (2,357 m)

⭐ *Summer facilities at Canyon Village: visitor center, ranger station, amphitheater, campground, post office, lodging, food service, general store, photo shop, service station, auto towing and repair, public showers, coin-operated laundry, horse rental.* **Winter facilities:** *warming hut, daytime snack bar, vending machines, snowmobile fuel.*

This section of road is the middle bar of the figure eight that forms the **Grand Loop Road.** A mature forest of lodgepole pines lines the first few miles, then gives way to a landscape of infant trees growing in the linear shadows of dead-standing and blackened trees from the 1988 fires.

Eight miles from **Canyon Junction**, the road cuts through **Virginia Meadows,** a painterly grassland of seasonal wildflowers—red Indian paintbrush, deep-blue fringed gentian, bright blue larkspur, yellow sunflowers, and lupines of every hue of purple. This wild garden is kept moist by nature's irrigator, a high water table; underground water is close to the surface here. Too wet for trees, Virginia Meadows supports these abundant wildflowers

The Gibbon River is a good place to hunt for western spotted frogs. MIKE SNYDER PHOTO

and lots of grass. The habitat is just right for the elk you may see grazing here in the early morning and evening.

The swift **Gibbon River** flows through Virginia Meadows on its way to **Virginia Cascade,** where the foaming water tumbles down 60 feet (1.8 m) inside the northwest edge of the **Yellowstone Caldera.** Hikers and bikers can view the cascade along a 3-mile (4.8 km) stretch of the old park highway.

The Gibbon is one river that is wholly contained within park boundaries. Its source is in the mountains around **Grebe Lake** and it ends at its confluence with the **Firehole River.** The Gibbon River supports mostly brook trout where it passes through Virginia Meadows.

Heading toward **Norris Junction,** the Grand Loop Road passes through part of a 22-mile (35.2 km) swath of trees that were tossed about like matchsticks when a microburst or wind shear skipped through this area in 1984. The felled trees became ready fuel for the fires of 1988, which burned the area so completely that only in recent years have forest plant species begun to really take hold again.

In a few more miles, the road joins the west side of the Grand Loop Road at Norris Junction.

Canyon Junction
to Tower-Roosevelt Junction

19 miles (31 km)
Elevation at Canyon Junction: 7,734 feet (2,357 m)

⭐ *Summer facilities at Canyon Village: visitor center, ranger station, amphitheater, campground, post office, lodging, food service, general store, photo shop, service station, auto towing and repair, public showers, coin-operated laundry, horse rental. Winter facilities: warming hut, daytime snack bar, vending machines, snowmobile fuel. The Grand Loop Road is closed to snowmobiling 4 miles (6.4 km) north of Canyon Junction. Summer facilities at Tower Fall: amphitheater, campground, general store.
Winter facilities: none.*

Steep grades and late snows discouraged most early tourists from tackling this portion of the **Grand Loop Road.** But in the 1920s, with the introduction of automobiles and paved roads, the going got much easier. Tourists ever since have added mountain scenery to their park itineraries.

The blur of unending lodgepole pines gives way to spruce and fir as the road climbs to **Dunraven Pass,** altitude 8,859 feet (2,700 m). Superintendent

Carry plenty of water and dress in layers for a moderate hike above the tree line to the summit of Mount Washburn.

If You Only Have Time for One Hike...

On a clear day, you really can almost see forever from the top of **Mount Washburn.** Before you stretches a vast panorama of all the park's mountain ranges, **Yellowstone Lake,** the **Hayden Valley,** the **Yellowstone River,** parts of the **Grand Canyon of the Yellowstone River,** even the **Grand Tetons** 100 miles (160 km) to the south.

From your perch on the edge of the giant **Yellowstone Caldera,** imagine how this scene looked 600,000 years ago. After the tremendous blast, lava rumbled up Mount Washburn's southern slope and gouged out half the mountain. Its momentum exhausted, the sludge flowed back to the central part of the park, adding to the rubble in the great crater. The lava's course put Mount Washburn at the northern edge of the Yellowstone Caldera, which stretches southward to include two-thirds of what is now Yellowstone Lake and a full quarter of Yellowstone National Park.

The summit of Mount Washburn offers a wide-angle view of Yellowstone, including the vegetative mosaic created by the fires of 1988. From here, you can see that the fires burned broad areas, but left others virtually untouched.

Access to the summit is via **Chittenden Road,** a spur designed by engineer Hiram Chittenden. He wanted to offer the park's first motorists a true mountain-climbing experience, as well as a spectacular view of the park. Today the road is closed to automobiles, but hikers are welcome. Both ends of the Chittenden Road offer an approach to the summit. Each is 3.2 miles (5.1 km) long and steadily climbs 1,400 feet (420 m) past an ever-changing vista of Engelmann spruce, Douglas-fir, lush wildflowers, and, at the windy summit, alpine buttercups and phlox. As you climb, look for evidence of the mountain's explosive past. Also watch for bighorn sheep, yellow-bellied marmots, golden-mantled ground squirrels, and rosy finches.

The southern trailhead is just below the pass at the **Dunraven Pass Picnic Area.** Limited parking is available. As you skirt fallen rocks and walk the knife-edged ridge just below the lookout, think of the intrepid motorists of 1915. Imagine driving or riding in a car, even a modern four-wheel-drive vehicle, over this byway!

The second approach to the summit of Mount Washburn has a completely different character. Used for servicing the lookout, this half of the Chittenden Road is wide and well maintained. It is an easier trek for small children and their nervous adult guardians. Bicycles are also permitted here. To access this trailhead, stop at the **Chittenden Road Parking Area** on the north side of **Dunraven Pass.**

No matter which approach you choose, remember that even on the hottest summer day, the summit will probably be icy cold. Carry extra clothing in your day pack. You might start the hike in shorts and a T-shirt and end up wearing long pants, a sweater, a windbreaker, a woolen hat, and mittens!

The Hard Rock Forest

Volcanic blasts 40 to 50 million years ago triggered huge mud landslides in the Yellowstone region. One such slide covered **Specimen Ridge.** The mudflows quickly knocked some trees flat and carried others upright for a short distance, then slowly choked and buried them in ash and mud. Both fallen and standing trees were petrified by hot water mixed with the dissolved silica from the ash, creating a potent solution that seeped into the open pores of the dead trees. This turned the trees, literally, to stone. Later, glaciers scoured the landscape, excavating some of the hard rock forest.

By taking a thin slice of petrified wood and dissolving the silica in it with acid, scientists can identify the woody fiber that remains. Thus we know that these petrified forests were made up of magnolia, walnut, oak, dogwood, hickory, and sequoia—trees that grow in a hot, humid climate like that found in the southeastern United States. How different from the Douglas-fir forest that grows today in Yellowstone's dry and seasonally frigid climate! If you'd like to step back in time, ask about an interpretive hike to Specimen Ridge at the **Horace M. Albright Museum and Visitor Center** at **Mammoth Hot Springs.**

P. W. Norris named the pass in 1879 for the Fourth Earl of Dunraven, Windham Thomas Wyndham-Quin, a one-man Chamber of Commerce. The earl's published account of his adventures in the West helped attract a flood of British and European tourists to Yellowstone.

The pass takes advantage of a gap in the **Washburn Range,** one of only two mountain ranges that are wholly contained within park boundaries. The other "local" range is the **Red Mountain Range,** south of **Yellowstone Lake** between **Lewis and Heart lakes.**

On the east side of the road is **Mount Washburn,** a volcano that erupted 50 million years ago and the main peak in the Washburn Range. Members of the 1870 Washburn-Langford-Doane exploring party voted unanimously to name the mountain after their leader, Henry D. Washburn, who made the first recorded ascent to the mountain's 10,243-foot (3,122 m) summit. Since that time, thousands of visitors have shared the 360-degree view from the top of Mount Washburn. Today's visitors can take a break from the peak's relentless chilling wind in an observation room beneath the fire lookout station.

As the Grand Loop Road descends from Dunraven Pass, look for the abundant evidence of new forest growth among the dead-standing lodgepole pines. A broad valley of grass and sagebrush opens below. Groves of shimmering aspen sprout up wherever water collects. Where the road folds back on itself, stop and use binoculars to scan for grizzly bears along the border between grassland and trees. This is prime grizzly habitat, closed to human encroachment.

What's in a Name?

Although its name seems altogether fitting, **Tower Fall** didn't come by it easily.

Humans have always felt a need to name things in their environment. Native Americans, mountain men, miners, and explorers all labeled Yellowstone's features. They chose words that identified the feature's characteristics, or the names of people who were in some way associated with the area. Most names were given casually, drawing on a visitor's first impression of a feature. Few attracted the feisty debate that accompanied the christening of **Tower Creek** and Tower Fall.

At the outset of their journey, members of the Washburn-Langford-Doane expedition agreed to refrain from naming any of the features they discovered after themselves or their friends. When the explorers came upon an unnamed creek that plummeted in a spectacular waterfall between slender towers, Walter Trumbull suggested the names "Minaret Creek" and "Minaret Fall." Samuel T. Hauser objected, claiming "Minaret" violated their agreement because Trumbull had a sweetheart named Minnie Rhett. Despite Trumbull's adamant denial that the name had personal implications, the party decided to play it safe with "Tower Creek" and "Tower Fall." Trumbull and some of his fellow explorers later speculated that Hauser had a sweetie by the name of Miss Tower, but, by then, the name "Tower" had stuck.

Despite their self-imposed rule, and on the very day they christened Tower Creek and Tower Fall, members of the Washburn party unanimously named **Mount Washburn** after their leader.

The names for the creek, the falls, and the mountain were made official when Yellowstone became our first national park. At the time, the task of assigning permanent names fell to the U.S. Geological Survey, led by Ferdinand V. Hayden. Hayden set down careful rules: to first adopt historic names, but if none existed, to choose names that reflected the park's natural resources and honored men who were linked with the park through science or politics. "Tower Creek," "Tower Fall," and "Mount Washburn" all passed muster.

To the east, across the **Grand Canyon of the Yellowstone River**, is **Specimen Ridge.** This is undoubtedly the area where Jim Bridger claimed he saw petrified animals and trees and such. He was right about the trees.

The Grand Loop Road continues its descent and arrives at **Tower Fall.** A footpath near the general store leads to a platform overlooking the 132-foot (40 m) Tower Fall, another dramatic example of water erosion. For a close-up look at the base of the falls, continue down the path another 0.5 mile (0.8 km), descending 300 feet (90 m). The "towers" are the products of basaltic lava that cooled and cracked in giant crystalline monoliths. **Tower Creek** wore away the glacial gravels and older volcanic rocks between these hexagonal columns to form the waterfall.

Beyond Tower Fall, the Grand Loop Road cuts beneath **Overhanging Cliff,** a conglomerate formation of lava and stream gravel that actually leans about 40 feet (12 m) over the road. Watch for white-throated swifts and a variety of swallows peeping out of their "high-rise apartments" in the cliff.

Just before **Tower-Roosevelt Junction,** the road passes the northernmost and narrowest part of the Grand Canyon of the Yellowstone River, appropriately called **The Narrows.** The canyon is 800 feet (240 m) deep at this spot and about 1,500 feet (450 m) wide. Look right inside the entrance to The Narrows for a thin stone column: **The Needle.** Wind and water have worn away the softer rock on the edges of this volcanic chimney. Hexagonal basalt columns make up the fencelike formation bordering The Narrows.

For another look at The Narrows, stop at **Calcite Springs** and take a short walk along the trail there. Watch for bighorn sheep, red-tailed hawks, and ospreys moving about in the canyon.

The Grand Loop Road soon reaches **Tower-Roosevelt Junction,**where it is joined by the **Northeast Entrance Road.**

Northeast Entrance
to Tower-Roosevelt Junction

* *

29 miles (47 km)
Elevation at Northeast Entrance: 7,365 feet (2,245 m)

⚙ *The road from* **Cooke City, Montana,** *to* **Mammoth Hot Springs** *is open year-round. The* **Beartooth Highway** *(U.S. Highway 212) and* **Chief Joseph Highway** *(Wyoming Highway 296) east of Cooke City are closed from about mid-October to the Friday of Memorial Day weekend, depending on weather and road conditions.* **Year-round facilities at the Northeast Entrance:** *ranger station.*

When you arrive at the **Northeast Entrance,** you will probably still be under the spell of the breathtaking **Beartooth Highway,** one of the most scenic drives in the country. The rugged beauty of the landscape continues nonstop as you pass through the gateway communities of **Cooke City** and **Silver Gate, Montana,** and enter the park.

The rustic native log construction of the **Northeast Entrance Ranger Station** (built in 1934–1935) was designed to blend with the environment. This bit of "parkitecture" earned the station designation as a National Historic Landmark.

The **Northeast Entrance Road** follows the old **Bannock Trail**, a route the Shoshone Bannock Indians used long ago to reach their ancestral hunting grounds in the north-central part of Yellowstone. The trail runs through the jagged **Absaroka Mountains,** passing between two of the park's highest peaks: **Abiathar Peak** at 10,928 feet (3,331 m) and **Barronette Peak** at 10,404 feet (3,171 m). Abiathar (pronounced uh-BI-uh-ther) Peak is named after Charles Abiathar White, a paleontologist who helped the U.S. Geological Survey in its western explorations during the 1860s and 1870s. Barronette Peak honors "Yellowstone Jack" Baronett, an adventurer, prospector, scout, and guide who built the first bridge over the **Yellowstone River.** "Baronett" was misspelled when the peak was officially named in 1878.

The road flanks **Soda Butte Creek** on down the valley. **Soda Butte,** a singular hot spring terrace, is 11 miles (17.6 km) in from the Northeast Entrance. When Soda Butte was active, it built up layer after layer of calcium carbonate, a kind of limestone similar to that found at **Mammoth Hot Springs.** Dissolved by hot underground water, the limestone bubbled to the surface in solution and settled out as it cooled, hardening once again.

About halfway to **Tower-Roosevelt Junction,** Soda Butte Creek joins the larger **Lamar River.** Take a break here and look for a well-worn path, a remnant of the Bannock Trail. If it is winter, you may spot bighorn sheep or any of the herds of bison and elk that live here throughout the year.

Arnold Hague, who in 1883 became chief of the U.S. Geological Survey's Yellowstone surveys, named the river to honor Lucius Quintus Cincinnatus Lamar. Lamar was Secretary of the Interior from 1885 to 1888, and Hague wrote of him: "[he] has done so much for the park."

The broad **Lamar Valley,** like the **Hayden Valley** in the central part of the park, was once covered with hundreds of feet of moving ice. The glaciers swept downhill from high in the surrounding mountains, pushing massive granitic boulders across the valley floor and breaking off huge chunks of valley ice.

When the glaciers finally receded more than 10,000 years ago, the boulders were left high and dry. They are now called glacial erratics. The silt-covered ice chunks melted, forming shallow ponds and lakes, or kettles. As in the Hayden Valley, the Lamar Valley's combination of glacial till and sediments forms an impermeable layer that will not permit much in the way of tree growth. Grasses and forbs grow in abundance, making the Lamar Valley another haven for wildlife.

Watch the Lamar River for waterfowl—Barrow's goldeneyes and mallard ducks. Cast a line for native Yellowstone cutthroat or nonnative rainbow and brook trout, or search a glacial kettle for frogs. The open, grassy meadows are a good place to look for pronghorns, bison, elk, and coyotes, too. The number and variety of wildlife frequenting the Lamar Valley made it a natural choice for the reintroduction of the gray wolf, also called the timber wolf.

Wolf-watching is a popular pastime in Yellowstone.

According to park biologist Doug Smith, the best way to see wolves in Yellowstone is from the road with binoculars or, better yet, with a spotting scope. The best time to see wolves is at daybreak, and the best place is in the Lamar Valley. How will you know where to look? Just stop where you see a crowd of people, Smith says.

The Northeast Entrance Road passes the **Lamar Ranger Station,** where the Army and, later, the National Park Service once raised bison to save them from extinction. Near the mouth of **Rose Creek,** the ranger station, horse barn, bunkhouse, and ranger residence are part of the **Lamar Buffalo Ranch Historic District,** and are listed on the National Register of Historic Places. The buildings were built in 1915, 1926, 1927, and 1937 respectively. The ranger station provides emergency services only.

The Lamar Valley still sports remnants of buffalo ranching days—irrigation ditches, fencing, and water troughs. The ranch no longer rounds up wild bison, but it is the home of the Yellowstone Institute and the Park Service's residential environmental education program, Expedition: Yellowstone! The Yellowstone Institute offers

Buffalo Ranching and Brucellosis

At one time, nearly 60 million bison roamed North America. They were a central part of the life and culture of native people, especially after horses became common in the 1600s. Native Americans used bison for making food, tools, clothing, and housing.

In the mid-1800s, white men shot bison by the hundreds for sport and for their hides and tongues. Later, the federal government hired hunters to kill the bison, in a calculated move to deny the Indians their livelihood and force them to move onto reservations. The railroads also hired bison hunters to clear the way for tracks as white development pushed west. By 1902, Yellowstone's herd of 23 bison was nearly the only one left on the continent.

Fearing the demise of Yellowstone's wild herd, the Army brought 21 domestic bison to the park from Montana and Texas. The soldiers tended these animals and bred them with the remaining wild bison in pens near **Mammoth Hot Springs.** Between 1907 and 1908, they moved the bison to the **Lamar Buffalo Ranch.** The careful efforts to rebuild the herd succeeded; the bison flourished. Until the 1960s, the park periodically culled bison to maintain a herd of 1,500 on the **Northern Range,** which includes the **Lamar and Yellowstone river valleys** from **Soda Butte** to the **North Entrance.**

Either cattle or domestic bison introduced brucellosis to the wild herd; no one knows which. The disease persists in park animals today, and it is causing a furor. Brucellosis can cause pregnant cattle, elk, or bison to abort their first calves, though it seems to have little impact on elk or bison. There is no cure for brucellosis, nor is there a suitable vaccine for bison. Brucellosis is transmitted primarily when noninfected animals come into direct contact with infected tissue or contaminated feed. No one has proven that bison can transmit brucellosis to domestic cattle on the open range; the disease has only been transmitted from bison to cattle under laboratory conditions. Still, the possibility exists, and livestock producers are up in arms about it.

A separate but related issue is how to manage the size of the park's bison herds. In 1968, the Park Service changed its policy of culling bison within the park to killing only those that wandered outside park boundaries. Park rangers shot three bulls in 1974 and one in 1978.

Aided by the policy of natural regulation within the park and a lack of natural predators, the bison herds continued to grow. By 1990, the park's bison population ballooned to 2,400, and the animals left the park in increasing numbers to find winter range. Livestock producers became increasingly concerned; more wandering bison meant a greater likelihood of their cattle getting brucellosis. Control measures just outside the park's northern and western boundaries claimed the lives of ever-higher numbers of bison. In the fall of 1994, after a series of mild winters, the northern herd peaked at about 4,000. By 1997, winter kill and management had reduced the herd by about half, to 2,200.

The presence of brucellosis and the annual harvest are issues that will not go away. Livestock producers have a lot at stake: Montana could lose its "brucellosis class-free status." Losing that status could mean exclusion from livestock marketing worldwide. However, many Americans can't countenance the fact that wild bison are being shot by the hundreds each winter. Bison continue to be the focus of heated and complex debate. The Park Service, federal and state wildlife and livestock agencies, and livestock producers are working overtime to find a solution.

a variety of seminars and camps to teach both adults and children more about the park. Participants stay in insulated, heated cabins, built with funds from the Yellowstone Association. The association sponsors the institute and manages book sales in the park's visitor centers and museums. To learn more about these programs, see page 117–118.

Directly south of the Lamar Ranger Station is **Specimen Ridge**. You can hike there from the ranger station. (For information on Specimen Ridge, see the "Canyon Junction to Tower-Roosevelt Junction" section of the guide.)

Slough Creek, renowned as a fine fishery for native cutthroat trout, runs near the Lamar Ranger Station. Next to the creek is a quiet campground. If you linger by the creek, watch for eagles soaring, picking up air currents off the rocky cliffs as they search for rodents.

A 4-mile (6.4 km) round-trip trail begins on a gravel access road in the campground, climbs through a forest of Douglas-fir, and finally drops into **Slough Creek Valley**, a place of aspens, open ponds, and lots of animals—moose, mule deer, elk, ducks, and coyotes.

Wolves

Forget what you have heard about The Big Bad Wolf. As Alexander T. Wolf insists in *The True Story of the Three Little Pigs*, "it's all wrong."

The "true" story about wolves is not exactly what author Jon Scieszka would have us believe in his children's picture book, but there is no denying wolves have gotten a bum rap. Their portrayal in fables and folklore has been almost universally negative. We have been taught that wolves are vicious and bloodthirsty, and that they attack humans. Our language gives voice to those negative vibes: "wolf whistle," "wolf down food," "wolf in sheep's clothing." No wonder the reintroduction of wolves in Yellowstone stirred up so much controversy!

Gray or timber wolves were a part of the Yellowstone scene for millennia, fulfilling their role in the balance of nature. Then in the late 1800s and early 1900s, park managers upset the balance. The 1872 act establishing Yellowstone as a national park declared the government "shall provide against the wanton destruction of the fish and game found within said Park." The park's managers decided that wolf predation of elk and bison was "wanton destruction," so from the park's inception, wolves were poisoned and shot. In 1923, the last pups were pulled from their den for extermination. The last confirmed sighting of a lone wolf was in 1936.

Enter the Endangered Species Act. Passed by Congress in 1973, the act required the U.S. Fish and Wildlife Service (USFWS) to restore missing species to places they once called home, wherever possible. National Park Service policy also called for the restoration of native species. And so a lengthy process began, kicked off in 1987 by the USFWS Northern Rocky Mountain Wolf Recovery Plan.

Reintroduction took nearly ten years, dozens of hearings, and thousands of letters. Livestock producers in Montana, Wyoming, and Idaho feared that wolves would decimate their herds. Some people worried that wolves would wipe out popular ungulate prey species like pronghorn, deer, elk, and bison. But the majority wanted a "missing link" restored to Yellowstone.

Finally in 1995, 60 years after the last wolf howled in Yellowstone, 14 gray wolves were captured in western Canada and released in Yellowstone. Seventeen more wolves were released the following year. At last, Yellowstone had all the species that were present at the park's inception.

A private fund administered by the Defenders of Wildlife provides compensation for livestock losses, of which there have been few. Biologists have radio-collared adult wolves to follow their movements, adding to the information base. Through careful monitoring, researchers can verify that the 85 to 90 wolves roaming freely in the park and wild parts of the Greater Yellowstone Ecosystem have not significantly impacted prey species. Wolves are opportunists. They kill young, old, or sick prey animals rather than healthy adults.

The gray wolf will be removed from the endangered species list when the USFWS reaches its recovery goal: ten self-sustaining wolf packs over three successive years in each of three recovery areas—northern Montana, Yellowstone National Park, and central Idaho. Wildlife biologists believe they will easily achieve that goal.

Along the way, watch for horse-drawn wagons traveling to and from the historic **Silver Tip Ranch.** Located just across the park boundary, this private ranch has been in operation since the early 1900s and has official permission for nonmotorized access.

As the Northeast Entrance Road approaches Tower-Roosevelt Junction, look closely at the trees. The branches closest to the ground have been stripped of their needles by winter-browsing deer and elk.

Tower-Roosevelt Junction to
Mammoth Hot Springs

• •

18 miles (29 km)
Elevation at Tower-Roosevelt Junction: 6,270 feet (1,911 m)

⊕ *Summer facilities at Tower-Roosevelt Junction: ranger station, lodging,*
food service, general store, service station, horse rental.
Winter facilities: ranger station.

For centuries, **Tower-Roosevelt Junction** was a crossroads for Indians, trappers, and explorers. President Theodore Roosevelt chose this junction as the jump-off point for a 16-day tour of the park in April 1903. He ended his visit by dedicating the basalt arch at the **North Entrance** outside **Gardiner, Montana.**

Riding on the coattails of the president's visit, a new concession, **Camp Roosevelt,** opened in 1906. Ten years later, **Roosevelt Lodge** was built in the trees just south of the junction. The lodge is listed on the National Register of Historic Places. Another historic structure, the **Tower Ranger Station,** is a 1923 reconstruction of an Army station built on the site in 1907.

Just after leaving Tower-Roosevelt Junction, take a 0.5-mile (0.8 km) side road to the **Petrified Tree,** the only one in the park that is close to a road. This stump is a remnant of a subtropical forest that grew here 40 to 50 million years ago. Like the petrified trees on **Specimen Ridge,** this redwood turned to stone after being smothered in volcanic ash. Two other tree stumps used to stand near this one, but early visitors carried them away. Remember: "Take only pictures, leave only footprints."

North of the Petrified Tree is **Yancey's (or Pleasant) Valley.** During the 1903 trip, President Roosevelt and writer-naturalist John Rice Burroughs rode horseback and camped in the valley for a week before boarding a sleigh to visit the geyser basins along the **Firehole River** and the **Grand Canyon of the Yellowstone River.** "Uncle" John Yancey kept crude accommodations for tourists who visited this area of the park and for miners headed east to the ore district around **Cooke City, Montana.** The **Pleasant Valley Hotel** and its outbuildings, constructed between 1884 and 1893, were demolished long ago, but park concessionaires still use this site for "Old West" cookouts.

Back on the **Grand Loop Road,** the forest begins to open up again. Rocky Mountain juniper and sagebrush tell us this country is dry. Only about 18 inches (45 cm) of snow and rain fall here each year. Despite the arid climate, open areas harbor many small lakes and ponds. Look closely and you will see where beavers have built their dams. The gnawed-off aspens and cottonwoods around the ponds are a giveaway. Also watch for ducks, geese, and swans.

Continue on the Grand Loop Road, and 3.5 miles (4.8 km) from Tower-Roosevelt Junction (north of **Elk Creek**), grooved and wrinkled **Garnet Hill** will come into view. Part of the **Beartooth batholith,** the hill is comprised of basement rock—the oldest rock on earth. True to its name, Garnet Hill contains imperfect garnets, which are volcanic gemstones.

A pullout offers a look at **Undine Falls** on **Lava Creek.** The watery staircase drops 50 feet (15 m) and lands in a froth at a rockslide. The rocks quiet the water and, once again, it slips easily downstream.

The Grand Loop Road winds for 3.5 more miles (5.6 km) before it meets the **North Entrance Road.** You will catch your first sight of the terraces of **Mammoth Hot Springs,** looming like ancient ruins.

North Entrance to Mammoth Hot Springs

5 miles (8 km)
Elevation at North Entrance: 5,314 feet (1,620 m)

✺ *Facilities at the North Entrance: none.*

Approaching the **North Entrance** from outside the park, you pass through **Gardiner, Montana.** You can't help but notice that the town ends abruptly at the crest of a hill on Front Street. And only one side of Front Street has any buildings because the park's northern border runs along the sidewalk. Across the street is a sagebrush flat where mule deer and pronghorn antelope play in the summer and bull elk and bison forage from late fall through winter. Elk frequently wander through Gardiner. In earlier days, poachers sometimes killed these "sightseers" and dragged them home under the cloak of darkness.

From the confluence of the **Gardner and Yellowstone rivers,** Front Street loops past the former Yellowstone Transportation Company buildings (now owned by AmFac Parks & Resorts) and other gateway businesses and passes under the **North Entrance (Roosevelt) Arch.** President Theodore Roosevelt, a park defender and an ardent conservationist, dedicated this 50-foot-high (15 m) structure in 1903. Stone for the stacked hexagonal basalt columns was quarried nearby. You can see basalt towers like these, but created by nature, at **Sheepeater Cliffs, Tower Fall, The Narrows,** and elsewhere around the park.

Gardner River is one of the oldest place names in the park. Mountain man John Gardner probably named the river after himself. From the mid-1830s on, other trappers called the river Gardner's Fork. A member of the 1870 Washburn party who heard Gardner's name mispronounced adopted the phonetic spelling "Gardiner" for the settlement.

The North Entrance is one of only two entrances to Yellowstone that offer year-round access to wheeled vehicles. The other—the **Northeast Entrance**—is only open to local travel during the winter because U.S. Highway 212 is not plowed beyond **Cooke City, Montana.** Of the five park approaches, the North Entrance is lowest in elevation and has the mildest climate. Only 13 inches (33cm) of rain and snow fall here each year.

The dryness accounts for the sagebrush. This arid, open country is perfect for pronghorns. In the summer, watch for them on your drive to **Mammoth Hot Springs.** And listen for meadowlarks calling to one another. In other seasons, you may see herds of elk, bison, mule deer, and bighorn sheep migrating to lower elevations in search of food. Abundant grass is visible above the snow here even in midwinter.

The **North Entrance Road** winds through **Gardner Canyon,** where the Gardner River tumbles past steep walls of unstable shales and sandstones. The rock was deposited by a shallow sea that covered the west-central part of North America about 90 million years ago, long before the volcanic activity that formed Yellowstone. In the steepest parts of the canyon, watch for bighorn sheep. Eagles, ospreys, dippers, and kingfishers hang out along the river. In spring, the winter's snowmelt supersaturates the canyon walls, so that they may slump and slide, sometimes blocking traffic. This is scenery in motion!

On the east side of the road 3.5 miles (5.6 km) from the North Entrance, a sign marks the **45th Parallel of Latitude,** an imaginary line exactly halfway between the equator and the North Pole.

Pull into the parking lot and follow a 0.5-mile (0.8 km) path to a naturally heated swimming hole where the **Boiling River** feeds the Gardner River. For most of its short 145-yard (130.5 m) course, the Boiling River runs underground through a travertine formation. Invalids once flocked to the river for its medicinal effects. Swimming in the runoff of the Boiling River is only allowed during the day, and is prohibited in the spring when high water makes every river hazardous. It is illegal to swim or soak in the thermal features themselves, anywhere in the park.

The water runs shallow and warm where the Boiling River meets the Gardner River near the 45th Parallel of Latitude.

Soon after crossing the 45th Parallel, the North Entrance Road enters **Wyoming,** then mounts one last hill before reaching Mammoth Hot Springs.

To the east as you climb the hill, a raw mountain of shale and sandstone rises abruptly into view. **Mount Everts** is layered with evidence of an ancient sea that filled the West nearly 100 million years ago. Earth movements thrust the sediments upward and tilted them sideways. Around 2 million years ago, the first Yellowstone eruption covered the mountain with lava. The hardened lava cap rock is more than 90 million years younger than the softer rock below.

Mount Everts was named for U.S. Assessor Truman Everts of the Washburn-Langford-Doane expedition, who earned the honor the hard way. On September 9, 1870, at **Yellowstone Lake,** Everts became separated from the other members of the expedition. On September 10, he broke his glasses and his horse ran off with nearly all of his possessions. Quite near-sighted and now on foot, Everts spent the next 37 days wandering around, hallucinating, starving, and freezing. He was finally found near the cut on **Blacktail Plateau Drive,** 7 miles (11.2 km) east of here, and never made it as far as the mountain that bears his name. Everts' story originally appeared in *Scribner's Monthly Magazine* and was published as *Lost in Yellowstone,* a book edited by Yellowstone historian Lee Whittlesey.

The North Entrance Road spirals up the hill, past the campground, and enters Mammoth Hot Springs.

Mammoth Hot Springs to
Norris Junction

● ●

21 miles (34 km)
Elevation at Mammoth Hot Springs: 6,239 feet (1,902 m)

⭐ *The **Grand Loop Road** is closed from the **Upper Terraces** to **Norris Junction** from about the first Monday in November to the third Friday in April. **Year-round facilities at Mammoth Hot Springs:** National Park Service headquarters, museum and visitor center, lodging, food service, campground, clinic, post office, general store. **Summer-only facilities:** amphitheater, photo shop, service station, horse rental. **Winter-only facilities:** snowmobile fuel.*

Gleaming white terraces loom just ahead. They are the visible expression of a thermal system that extends all the way from these ruin-like formations, across the grassy field before you, to the **Boiling River** on the **45th Parallel of Latitude.** This massive thermal complex we call **Mammoth Hot Springs** has been active for thousands of years. Constantly changing in character, constantly spilling its endless supply of hot water, Mammoth has always been a jumping-off point for visitors to the park.

Early entrepreneurs recognized there was money to be made at Mammoth Hot Springs. Harry R. Horr spied the springs as he searched for Truman Everts and, in 1871, he returned with James McCartney. Horr and McCartney set up a crude spa that catered to invalids who camped, soaked, and drank the mineralized water. Horr claimed credit for naming Mammoth Hot Springs to indicate the great size of this thermal complex.

The lower elevation made it easy to reach and pleasant to visit year-round. This caught the attention of early park superintendent P. W. Norris. Norris praised Mammoth's "nearness and accessibility throughout the year, through one of the . . . main entrances to the Park . . . as well as accessibility to the other prominent points of interest in the Park." In 1879, Norris built Yellowstone's first park headquarters on **Capitol Hill,** a low glacial promontory just east of the hot springs terraces. The hill received its moniker because it was the center of authority in the park.

When the Army took over the administration of the park in 1886, the soldiers turned Norris's headquarters into private quarters and set up a temporary tent outpost and called it **Camp Sheridan.** Five cold winters later, the Army realized its presence would be needed for quite some time. The soldiers began building a permanent post, **Fort Yellowstone,** and in 1909 razed Norris's building on Capitol Hill. When the Army left the park in 1916, the chimneyed, red-roofed stone and tan frame buildings found new life as **Yellowstone National Park Headquarters.**

The Northern Elk Herd

Overhunting once threatened elk, just as it threatened bison. Until 1883, when hunting in Yellowstone was outlawed, hunters slaughtered elk by the thousands for their meat, their hides, and their ivory teeth. An elk has two canine teeth, the "ivories," that are prized for their value as jewelry. Early members of the Elk's Club used elk teeth for stickpins and cufflinks.

When the U.S. Army Cavalry arrived in the park in 1886, the soldiers cracked down on poachers and started protecting Yellowstone as a wildlife refuge. The elk also benefitted from an aggressive predator control program that eventually eradicated gray wolves from the park. Elk once again flourished in Yellowstone.

Between 1921 and 1929, the elk population continued to grow. In the 1930s, scientists and park managers decided that the **Northern Range** had exceeded its carrying capacity (the maximum number of animals that a particular habitat can support). To re-create a balance between the herds and their habitat, the Park Service adopted a variety of control measures. Between 1935 and 1968, park personnel transplanted elk, along with bison and pronghorn antelope, to areas beyond the boundaries of Yellowstone. For a time, park personnel culled elk inside the park and private hunters killed others when the elk left the park to seek winter range.

Then, in the 1960s, new studies suggested that ungulate populations could be self-regulating. The Park Service reversed its policies and once again protected the elk. In the 1980s, the expanding Northern Range elk herd began migrating to new winter range at the lowest park elevations and outside the park north of **Gardiner, Montana.** To ease the pressure on private lands, the Rocky Mountain Elk Foundation enabled the state of Montana and the USDA Forest Service to purchase 11,000 acres (4,400 ha) of winter range adjacent to the park.

Today, no trapping or hunting occurs in Yellowstone, and elk are once again the park's most numerous grazing animal. About 30,000 animals in seven or eight herds summer in the park, and 15,000 to 22,000 elk stay on in the winter. Yellowstone's elk population is now controlled by the amount of food available, by harsh winter weather, and by hunting outside the park in areas where the elk migrate.

The Army's former Bachelor Officers' Quarters now house the **Horace M. Albright Museum and Visitor Center** (named after Yellowstone's first Park Service superintendent), the **Yellowstone Park Research Library and Archives,** and the park's interpretive services. A double barracks behind the visitor center houses administrative offices, and more barracks provide space for the Yellowstone lending library and other park offices. Some park personnel live in the large stone and clapboard former officers' quarters along **Officers' Row.** A walking tour through the **Fort Yellowstone Historic District** begins in front of the Albright Visitor Center.

The Horace M. Albright Museum is open year-round at Mammoth Hot Springs.

All of the buildings at Mammoth sit atop an old hot spring terrace, which some early visitors thought might cave in at any moment. Rudyard Kipling, author of *The Jungle Book and Just So Stories,* observed that "[t]he ground rings as hollow as a kerosene-tin, and someday the **Mammoth Hotel,** guests and all, will sink into the caverns below and be turned into a stalactite." Remember Kipling's words as you wander around the Mammoth development. Across from the park concessions, notice the sinkholes on what was once the military parade ground.

If you are lucky enough to visit Yellowstone in the fall or winter, you will see elk strolling on the sidewalks of park headquarters and browsing in the yards of park employees. The residents put up temporary fences everywhere to protect shrubs, but the elk, drawn to the irrigated landscaping, often outwit these deterrents. The animals you see have become accustomed to humans, but they are not tame. Bull elk can be very aggressive during the rut (mating season), and cows with calves are often edgy in the spring. Do not approach elk, or any wildlife, at any time of year.

The 5-mile (8 km) **Beaver Ponds Loop Trail** is not easy to find, but well worth the effort of looking. Go south on the **Grand Loop Road** toward **Norris Geyser Basin.** Just before **Liberty Cap**—an extinct hot spring cone at the base of the Lower Terraces—you will find the trailhead tucked behind the garage next to the last stone house on your right. In the summer, the Beaver Ponds Loop can be hot and dry, so make sure you take plenty of water.

An extinct hot spring, Liberty Cap welcomes visitors at the base of the Lower Terraces.

The trail follows the creek up **Clematis Gulch,** quickly climbing 350 feet (105 m) through Douglas-firs. A long traverse through open meadows of sage and clusters of aspen leads to the beaver ponds, which are 2.5 miles (4 km) from the trailhead. Along the way, you may see elk, mule deer, pronghorns, moose, and, of course, beaver dams and lodges. Visitors seldom spot the beavers themselves, since these animals go about their business at night.

From the beaver ponds, the trail follows the broad, graveled **Old Gardiner Road,** which offers good views of **Mount Everts** to the east and **Sheep Mountain** to the north. The trail ends behind **Mammoth Hot Springs Hotel,** but you can follow the paved road in front of the commercial buildings back to the trailhead near Liberty Cap.

Liberty Cap stands 37 feet (11.1 m) tall and is 20 feet (6 m) thick at its base. Hot water once flowed from an opening at the top of the cone, depositing layers of travertine (a type of limestone), which formed the cone's peak. The deposits finally choked off the water, leaving this monumental cone. It reminded the 1871 Hayden survey party of the "liberty caps" worn by Colonial patriots during the American Revolution.

Across the Grand Loop Road from Liberty Cap and poised above the end of a residential street, **Opal Spring** is beginning to encroach on the **Reamer House.** Opal Spring is a blister on the lower slope of Capitol Hill, where the first park headquarters stood. Long dormant, Opal Spring sprang to life in 1926 and began oozing toward the house. A tennis court was removed in 1947; more recent years have seen the addition of an earthen wall and sandbags.

An example of prairie architecture, the Reamer House is listed on the National Register of Historic Places. Architect Robert Reamer designed the house in 1908. Reamer also designed the **Old Faithful Inn** and the **Roosevelt Arch** at the park's North Entrance, and he directed the renovation of the **Lake Hotel.** The juxtaposition of the Reamer House and Opal Spring illustrates the dilemma created by the Park Service mission to protect both natural and cultural resources.

Take the looping boardwalk around the many features of the **Lower Terraces.** Mammoth Hot Springs is constantly changing. If you have visited here before, you will probably notice a difference in the landscape. "Old friends" may have dried up or lost their color.

To reach the **Upper Terrace,** drive 1.5 miles (2.4 km) south from the visitor center on the road toward **Norris Junction.** Take the one-way **Upper Terrace Loop** another 1.5 miles (2.4 km) through a variety of active and inactive hot springs. The Park Service prohibits vehicles longer than 25 feet (7.6 m) along this narrow, winding road. Trails, varying from gentle to steep, descend from a parking lot to the Lower Terraces.

Back on the Grand Loop Road, traveling toward Norris Junction, you will pass a cut in the mountains called **Golden Gate.** Here, the road perches

Nature's Miner

The only thing that doesn't change about **Mammoth Hot Springs** and their deposits is the amount of water the hot springs expel. About 500 gallons (1,892.5 l) of hot water flush from the various hot springs every minute of every day, year-round. You are watching nature's miner at work. The hot water turns the hillside inside out, bringing more than 2 tons (1.8 mt) of dissolved limestone to the surface each day—the equivalent weight of four average-sized horses.

As the water evaporates, the limestone hardens as travertine, Layer by layer, about 8 inches (20 cm) of new travertine are added to the Mammoth terraces each year. The soft limestone here dissolves more easily than the volcanic materials found in the geyser basins, where sinter formations grow at infinitesimal rates.

How does the underground limestone become above-ground travertine? Rainwater seeps into the porous limestone of an ancient seabed under Mammoth's terraces. The water flows along fractures where it is heated, and picks up carbon dioxide. The "water" is now carbonic acid. As this hot, acidic groundwater percolates through the buried limestone beds, it dissolves rock and picks up lime (calcium carbonate) in solution. The now lime-bearing hot water eventually bubbles up to the surface, where a sudden decrease in pressure releases the carbon dioxide to the atmosphere. The lime settles out as travertine, a white rock similar to marble. Tiny bacteria and algae grow on and add color to the new rock.

The constant flow of hot water and the travertine it deposits keep the terraces ever-changing. Trees, ancient terraces, and other obstacles on the slope of the hill often force the runoff in new directions. If the water and sediments have nowhere to go, they eventually plug their own vents. When that happens, the water that fed those features is forced to surface elsewhere, forming a new hot springs. The eternal shifting of hot water channels and mineral loads creates a living sculpture.

While the water at Mammoth is plenty warm, it is not hot enough to form geysers. By drilling into the springs, scientists with the U.S. Geological Survey found the underground water temperature to be about 170 degrees F (73°C). Compare that to the temperatures at **Norris Geyser Basin,** where the surface water is 199 degrees F (93°C) and the underground water is 459 degrees F (237°C).

Mammoth Hot Springs is pretty far north of the great **Yellowstone Caldera,** but it still benefits from the area's central heat source, a fault line and a system of small radial fissures that emanate from the fault connecting Mammoth to Norris.

on the side of a lava cliff from Yellowstone's first eruption 2 million years ago. Yellow lichens cling to the bare rock.

Take a look at the lone vertical rock beside the guardrail. When roadbuilders wanted to widen the old road through Golden Gate, this rock stood in the way. Local sentiment and the park's photographer opposed pitching the rock unceremoniously into the canyon along with other obstacles.

Mineralized water creates a stairstep pattern as it flows from its source beneath Mammoth Hot Springs.

Roadbuilder Hiram Chittenden finally gave in. He assured the photographer that the key element of his many photographs would be spared: "[The rock] is now five feet higher, five feet farther to the front, and five feet farther from the cliff than it used to be; yet no one would suspect that it stands on a man-made pedestal instead of the one which nature provided."

Opposite Golden Gate to the east is **Bunsen Peak,** an 8,564-foot (2,623 m) mountain that may be the neck of a volcano from the Absaroka eruptions of about 50 million years ago. Bunsen Peak honors Robert Wilhelm Eberhard von Bunsen, an eminent German physicist, inventor, and chemist who studied geysers in Iceland. The bunsen burner was also named for von Bunsen.

For a sweeping view of the northern end of the park, take a 4-mile (6.4 km) round-trip hike to the top of Bunsen Peak. The trailhead is 5 miles (8 km) south of Mammoth Hot Springs, across the Grand Loop Road from **Swan Lake Flat.** Park and follow the old **Bunsen Peak Road** and watch for trail markers leading up the slope to your left. The trail climbs 1,300 feet (390 m) through sagebrush and pines burned by the 1988 fires. From the summit, you can see Swan Lake Flat, the **Blacktail Plateau,** the **Gallatin Mountain Range,** and the **Yellowstone River Valley.**

Swan Lake Flat is a dry area, but it gets more than one and a half times as much rainfall as Gardiner at the park's **North Entrance.** Trumpeter swans and other water birds often visit the shallow **Swan Lake** and the other glacial kettles and marshes. The ponds and gray-green sagebrush also attract pronghorns, elk, and bison.

Three miles (4.8 km) farther down the Grand Loop Road from Swan Lake Flat and Bunsen Peak Road, a short spur leads to **Sheepeater Cliff.** Superintendent P. W. Norris named the cliff in 1879 to honor the Sheepeater Indians, the only Native Americans known to have lived year-round in Yellowstone. The ancient Sheepeaters never had horses or rifles, but they did fashion formidable weapons and tools from the glasslike obsidian they quarried nearby. With sharp spears and arrowheads, they hunted Rocky Mountain bighorn sheep, deer, elk, and moose, animals that summered in this area to escape the insects and heat of lower elevations. The Sheepeaters softened ram horns in the area's thermal features to make bows for hunting. To learn more about these people, read *Moho Wat: Sheepeater Boy Attempts a Rescue* by Kenneth Thomasma. Thomasma is a master at weaving historical facts into a good story.

Sheepeater Cliff is formed by "picket fence" columns of basalt, similar to those that support the Roosevelt Arch at the North Entrance. The **Gardner River** makes this spot even more picturesque; it is a lovely spot for a quiet picnic.

Just after the turnoff to Sheepeater Cliff, the Grand Loop Road passes a Park Service campground along **Indian Creek.** A warming hut here provides winter shelter for skiers and snowmobilers.

In the summer, Indian Creek offers rustic camping and, in the winter, a warming hut for winter visitors. LAURA SNYDER PHOTO

As you travel, notice the downed and dead-standing timber where the 1988 fires burned on both sides of the Grand Loop Road, and the green corridor that was spared. You are in the midst of a fire mosaic.

Just south of Sheepeater Cliff, look for moose in **Willow Park.**

Two miles (3.2 km) from Willow Park, stone steps on the east side of the Grand Loop Road lead to **Apollinaris Spring**. The cold mineral water spring was an oasis for thirsty travelers in the 1880s. An early tourist named the spring after Apollinaris Water, a commercially bottled water. While a cool drink may sound appealing, wildlife have since contaminated the spring—so don't drink the water!

As the Grand Loop Road follows **Obsidian Creek,** Yellowstone's thermal nature becomes evident once again. Small, unmarked hot springs dot the creek bottom. You can explore this quiet area, but stay on the trails. Even small hot springs can cause serious injuries, or even fatalities.

Four miles (6.4 km) beyond Obsidian Cliff is a dead-looking hill called **Roaring Mountain.** Scientists with the U.S. Geological Survey named this barren hill in 1885 for the "shrill, penetrating sound of the

The Mountain of Glass

• • • • • • • • • • • • • • • • • • • •

A couple of miles beyond **Apollinaris Spring,** the **Grand Loop Road** brings you to **Obsidian Cliff,** made famous as Jim Bridger's "glistening mountain of glass." The rugged fur trapper and guide explored Yellowstone country in the 1830s and told tall tales about its many wonders. Superintendent P. W. Norris took note of Bridger's description when he named the cliff in 1878; however, researchers now believe the mountain Bridger discovered was actually located in southeast Wyoming.

Moss and lichens cover most of this ancient 150- to 200-foot (45–60 m) rock face, but Obsidian Cliff deserves a closer look. Black, shiny rock gleams under the vegetative blanket.

Obsidian Cliff was created by molten lava that cooled quickly—too quickly to form the crystals that are found in lava elsewhere in the park. Some scientists think the lava may have hit a glacier. That would cool it down fast!

Sheepeaters and other Indians quarried the glasslike obsidian rock to make sharp arrowheads, knives, and scrapers. They used these tools and they also traded them; some have been found as far away as Ohio. The importance of this quarry to these early people earned Obsidian Cliff recognition as a National Historic Landmark in 1966.

The Park Service has closed the trails along Obsidian Cliff to the public because of concerns about both visitor safety and vandalism. If you see obsidian chips around the base of the cliff, leave them in place. Protect your park by leaving all rocks where you find them, and urge other visitors to do the same.

steam constantly escaping from one or more vents located near the summit." Superheated earth from hidden thermal features killed its lodgepole pine forest. Acid from the steam emanating from the fumaroles bleached and crumbled the rocks. The mountain roared intermittently until the mid-1920s, when it became quiet, emitting only a few puffs of steam here and there. In July 1996, fumaroles developed all over the mountain. Today, Roaring Mountain looks like it is on fire once more.

Just before Norris Junction, **Norris Soldier Station** sits on the north bank of the **Gibbon River.** Built in 1886 to house lonely soldiers who patrolled the remote region on horseback and skis, the station is one of the longest-occupied outposts in the park. The original structure was replaced in 1897 and modified in 1908. When the National Park Service took over park management in 1916, the Norris Soldier Station became a ranger station and residence. It remained in use until it was damaged in the 1959 **Hebgen Lake** earthquake. The restored ranger station now houses the **Museum of the National Park Ranger,** which tells the story of how the duties of park rangers have changed over the years.

A small campground nearby has been popular for at least 10,000 years. Archaeologists found campfire remnants, obsidian flakes and chips, and bone fragments here and along a trail that leads from this campground to Obsidian Cliff.

Norris Junction to Madison Junction

14 miles (23 km)
Elevation at Norris Junction: 7,484 feet (2,281 m)

⊗ *Summer facilities at Norris Junction: museum, ranger station, bookstore, amphitheater, campground. **Winter facilities:** none.*

The **Grand Loop Road** reaches the middle bar of its figure-eight shape at **Norris Junction,** where a short spur road leads west to **Norris Geyser Basin.** During his park tenure from 1877 to 1882, the second superintendent, Philetus W. Norris, extensively explored and reported on Yellowstone's features. He named this basin, as well as many other park features, for himself. Not all of the names were adopted by the U.S. Geological Survey, but this one was, since Norris was gravely ill when he made the request and died a few months later.

The museum at Norris Geyser Basin is one of Yellowstone's original trailside museums. Built in 1929–1930, the **Norris Geyser Basin Museum** became a prototype for many national park buildings throughout the United States. In Yellowstone, the museums at **Fishing Bridge** and **Madison Junction** share its familiar stone and log construction. All three museums are National Historic Landmarks.

A breezeway between the wings of the Norris museum frames **Porcelain Basin,** one of the geyser basin's three main areas. Stairs and boardwalks descend to this colorful, steamy flat. A Yellowstone Association bookstore continues the "parkitecture" theme. Its telephones remain operable in the winter.

Norris is the hottest and most dynamic geyser basin in North America and, perhaps, the world. Scientists have measured temperatures of 459 degrees F (237°C) just 1,087 feet (326 m) beneath the surface. New hot springs and geysers come to life overnight, sometimes lasting months or years, sometimes becoming dormant in just a few days. Norris is also the oldest of Yellowstone's active geyser basins, the result of "location, location, location," which might be how a realtor would describe the unique setting that has allowed hot water to flow here for more than 115,000 years.

Norris Geyser Basin is at the intersection of two major fault lines or rock fractures, one that runs south from **Mammoth Hot Springs** and another that extends east from **Hebgen Lake,** near the park's western boundary. These breaks in the earth's crust collide at Norris Geyser Basin, where they are pierced again by fractures radiating from the great **Yellowstone Caldera** that has dominated central Yellowstone for 600,000 years. As a result of this

Get in on the action at Echinus Geyser!

cataclysmic junction, water from Yellowstone's abundant precipitation easily percolates downward through cracks and fissures. Little more than 0.6 to 1.8 miles (1–3 km) below the earth's surface, magma heats the water, forcing it to the surface as geysers, hot springs, mud pots, or fumaroles. Most of Norris Geyser Basin's thermal features release boiling water—that is, water that is at least 199 degrees F (93°C), which is the boiling point for this elevation.

If you have visited Mammoth Hot Springs, you will notice right away that something about Norris is different. The cones and terraces here are made of spiny geyserite or sinter, rather than the beady travertine you may have seen at Mammoth. Sinter is a product of highly acidic volcanic silica. The silica dissolves in the underground hot water system and bubbles up to the surface. At Mammoth Hot Springs, hot water circulates through and dissolves the limestone of ancient seabeds; when the water spills over, it deposits alkaline travertine. So hot springs are what they eat: the kinds of rock they bubble up through and dissolve determine the kinds of deposits they make. The majority of the earth's rare acid geysers are found at Norris Geyser Basin.

WARNING: Protect your eyeglasses and camera lenses from the geyser spray. Wipe them off immediately if they get wet. Silica bonds with glass and is nearly impossible to remove. After all, silica is an essential ingredient in the production of glass.

Depending on when you visit, you may hear about a basin-wide phenomenon that happens at Norris. Usually in late summer or early fall, many of the basin's hot springs and geysers suddenly become muddy—no matter how much precipitation Norris has received that year. Water levels and acidity fluctuate, water temperatures and colors change, and pools that are normally quiet spring to life and become powerful geysers. After a few days or a few weeks (remember, geysers aren't all that predictable), most features return to "normal" activity and the water runs clear once again. The reason for the basin-wide disturbance remains a mystery, but some scientists speculate that fluctuations in the complex underground reservoirs may be the cause.

Be sure to stop at the Norris museum and ask the ranger-naturalist what's new in the geyser basin and when some of the more permanent geysers may erupt. Then visit two of the basin's distinct areas: Porcelain Basin and **Back Basin.** The Park Service discourages travel in Norris's third area, **One Hundred Springs Plain,** because it has no established trails, and the terrain is acidic, hollow, and dangerous. Paths to the other basins begin at the museum.

A 0.75-mile (1.2 km) trail through Porcelain Basin illustrates why this area epitomizes change. Even the biggest, longest-living geysers are never quite the same from one year to the next. Small, short-lived geysers—spouters—spring up all the time, constantly sput-sput-sputtering water a few feet in the air until they seal themselves off with their own dissolved minerals. When this happens, the hot water in these tiny geysers is once again under pressure, and it has to find new pipelines to the surface. Traveling upward via new channels, the water explodes again as new spouters somewhere else.

The cloudy blue color that is so prevalent in Porcelain Basin is the result of very hot water holding silica in suspension. The color reminded Superintendent Norris of fine china, and it is why he named the area Porcelain Basin.

In midsummer, Porcelain Basin can feel like a frying pan. Fortunately, it is rimmed by groves of lodgepole pines where you can find shady relief. But approach the woody shelter carefully and quietly; the park's wildlife may be seeking a break from the heat, too.

The lodgepole pine forest at Norris is in constant flux, retreating here and there as underground heat increases, and advancing where thermal activity diminishes. The Back Basin is more wooded than Porcelain Basin and is especially inviting on a hot day. A 1.5-mile (2.4 km) trail leads to dozens of features, including two of Yellowstone's most famous geysers, **Steamboat** and **Echinus**.

There is something else that is special about Norris Geyser Basin: sagebrush lizards! Norris is one of the few areas in Yellowstone where these tiny reptiles can survive. The basin's warm earth and abundant insects provide ideal habitat for these cold-blooded predators. Their bodies are narrow and only 1.5 to 2 inches (3.8–5.1 cm) long, enabling them to quickly hide in rock piles, brush, or rodent burrows if danger threatens. Even though sagebrush lizards feed during the day, don't expect to see one as you explore Norris Geyser Basin. They are shy critters.

Heading south from Norris Junction toward Madison Junction, the Grand Loop Road follows the **Gibbon River**. Members of the second Hayden survey in 1872 named the river for General John Gibbon, who explored this area with his soldiers while on duty at **Fort Ellis**, near **Bozeman, Montana**. The road crosses a grassy meadow aptly named **Elk Park**. Watch for elk in the early morning or evening.

An often overlooked trail 4.5 miles (7.2 km) south of Norris leads to the brightly colored **Artists' Paint Pots**. The easy boardwalk-and-dirt path meanders for 1 mile (1.6 km), first across the south end of **Gibbon Meadows,** then through a partially burned forest. A short loop at the end of the trail shows off some of the most colorful hot springs and mud pots in this part of the park, along with some small geysers. Like other thermal features throughout Yellowstone, the paint pots take their color from dissolved minerals and hot water algae and bacteria. Other meadow trails lead to three fragile and dangerous backcountry thermal areas, which the Park Service discourages visiting.

Another 0.5 mile (0.8 km) down the road, just across the **Gibbon River Bridge,** another short trail leads to yet another unique area. The 2-mile

Thermal All-Stars

Steamboat Geyser (also called **New Crater Geyser**) is the tallest active geyser in the world—when it erupts. "When" is the operative word, since Steamboat's major eruptions occur without much warning and without any pattern scientists can detect. The interval between eruptions could be four days, or it could be fifty years! When Steamboat explodes, as it did on May 2, 2000, it throws water over 300 feet (90 m) into the air for anywhere from three to forty minutes. In 1878, Steamboat erupted for the Hayden survey party, making a powerful roar that reminded the explorers of an "old style paddle wheel steamboat." Following a major eruption, powerful jets of steam burst forth from the geyser for hours. The May 2000 steam plume reached 500 feet (150 m). More often, Steamboat ejects water 10 to 40 feet (3–12 m) in the air in frequent bursts.

Cistern Spring is linked to Steamboat Geyser underground. Normally a beautiful blue pool with constantly overflowing water, Cistern drains during a major eruption of its companion geyser. Cistern's abundant hot water brings up and deposits as much as 0.5 inch (12 mm) of grayish sinter each year. In contrast, **Old Faithful** (which is more in line with most of Yellowstone's thermal features) builds deposits at the rate of 0.5 to 1 inch (12–25 mm) per century!

Take a ringside seat near **Echinus Geyser** and watch the area's largest predictable geyser "up close and personal." Benches line three sides of the runoff area, since Echinus always draws a crowd. And it puts on a great show, erupting 40 to 60 feet (12–18 m) in the air every 35 to 70 minutes.

The best seat in the house is in the mini-grandstand above the crater. If you choose that seat, pick a rock near the top of the crater and keep your eye on it as Echinus slowly refills between eruptions. Then watch what happens to your rock as the geyser play begins, eventually swamping your rock and splashing water up and over the sides of the crater. Depending on the wind and where you are seated, you are liable to get wet when Echinus erupts, so protect your camera lens and eyeglasses. Eruptions usually last 6 to 14 minutes, but may last 60 minutes or more. Your rock will reappear as Echinus gurgles and drains clockwise after its eruption and immediately begins to refill.

The geyser reminded Albert C. Peale, a mineralogist with the 1878 Hayden survey, of spiny sea urchins in the genus *Echinus*. Its spiky sinter is produced by waters that are nearly as acidic as vinegar. Echinus is one of the world's largest acid-water geysers.

(3.2 km) round-trip hike to **Monument Geyser Basin** starts out easy, then climbs 500 feet (150 m) in 0.5 mile (0.8 km) to an assortment of dormant geyser cones. Park historian Lee Whittlesey writes that Monument Geyser Basin is "one of the strangest spots in the Park," noting its sculpted "gravestone-like thermal features." A similar impression inspired Superintendent Norris's name for the basin. Other thermal features here include the active **Thermos Bottle Geyser** and a number of mud pots, sulfur pools, and steam vents. A ranger-naturalist cautions hikers about the steep trail through Monument Geyser Basin: "Footing is on eroding geyserite and rhyolite, somewhat reminiscent of ball bearings."

Continue on the Grand Loop Road for another 0.5 mile (0.8 km) to one of the hottest springs in Yellowstone. **Beryl Spring** is named for its blue-green color, reminiscent of the gemstone beryl (pronounced "burl"). You are now 5.5 miles (8.8 km) south of Norris Geyser Basin.

Also stop at **Gibbon Falls,** where the water tumbles 84 feet (26 m) over the rim of the Yellowstone Caldera. Just before the falls, the Gibbon River is grassy-banked and only ankle deep. Then the water crashes over the brink in thundering white sheets to a pool below, where it turns placid once again.

As you watch the falls, golden-mantled ground squirrels and bright-eyed chipmunks may pester you. Please don't feed any of the park's wildlife. Junk-food junkies can't stay healthy for long in the wild. They become too dependent on human foods and may stop eating their natural diets.

Terrace Springs, with its gorgeous algal colors, is just off the Grand Loop Road 0.25 mile (0.4 km) before Madison Junction. Across the road is a 6-mile (9.6 km) round-trip trail to the top of **Purple Mountain.** The trail ascends some 1,500 feet (450 m) through the mosaic burn of a lodgepole pine forest. From Purple Mountain's summit at 8,433 feet (3,530 m), you can see where the Gibbon and **Firehole rivers** converge to form the **Madison River.** You can get to the trailhead from the campground at Madison Junction, where the Grand Loop Road joins the **West Entrance Road.**

how
YOU CAN HELP

. . . .

Any activity that occurs in the Greater Yellowstone Ecosystem is intricately tied to the park's abundant natural resources. These resources need our help. Learn as much as you can about the geothermal features, plants, and animals of the park and the land around it. No matter what your age, you can do your part to help Yellowstone National Park.

Grade school students can attend one of several special programs offered by the National Park Service Environmental Education Office.

- For a nominal fee, children ages five to twelve can sign on at any park visitor center as Junior Rangers. Participants earn Junior Ranger patches by completing a series of activities explained in a Park Service handout. Eleven thousand children earn patches each year.

- Fourth through eighth grade classes may compete by lottery to take part in the residential environmental education program, Expedition: Yellowstone! Selected classes spend three to five days at the historic Buffalo Ranch in the Lamar Valley. Both spring and fall sessions are offered. Fee-based and self-supporting, Expedition: Yellowstone! serves 900 students annually.

- A grant-supported summer program, Exploring Yellowstone, serves grade school students from Mammoth Hot Springs and from Gardiner, Cooke City, and Corwin Springs, Montana.

For more information about any of these programs, contact the Environmental Education Office, P.O. Box 168, Yellowstone National Park, Wyoming 82190; 307-344-7381; TDD 307-344-2386. On the Internet, look for the park's website at http://www.nps.gov/yell.

As for the rest of us, we can do a lot, too.

- Visit the park and attend talks by, or go hiking with, ranger-naturalists.

- Read one or more of the excellent books listed in the Bibliography.

- Follow stories about the Greater Yellowstone Ecosystem in national magazines and in your local newspaper.

- Rent a film or videotape from the Yellowstone National Park Film Library. Film subjects include wildlife, U.S. history, the environment, and other topics pertaining to Yellowstone. Write, phone, or e-mail the park's Environmental Education Office for details.

- Participate in educational field programs conducted by the nonprofit Yellowstone Institute. For more than 20 years, the Yellowstone Institute has offered courses, some for college credit, on the park's flora, fauna, geothermal resources, and folklore. For more information, or to receive a free catalog, contact the Yellowstone Institute, P.O. Box 117, Yellowstone National Park, Wyoming 82190; 307-344-2294. Read about it on the web at http://www.yellowstoneassociation.org/yellinst.htm.

• Join a nonprofit organization dedicated to supporting Yellowstone and/or its ecosystem. The organizations listed below have all been recognized by the National Park Service as park protectors. Each plays an important role in preserving Yellowstone's natural and human resources. Donations are tax-deductible.

Since 1933, the **Yellowstone Association** has provided educational services and funding for special park projects through its retail sales in Yellowstone's visitor centers and through the mail. The association also sponsors the Yellowstone Institute. For more information, contact the Yellowstone Association, P.O. Box 117, Yellowstone National Park, Wyoming 82190; 307-344-2296. Or look up the association on the web at http://www.YellowstoneAssociation.org.

Working closely with the National Park Service, the **Yellowstone Park Foundation** provides funding to augment and, in some cases, solely support habitat restoration, wildlife management, historical and cultural interpretation, and research projects that would not otherwise be possible because of shrinking government appropriations. To find out how you can help the foundation help the park, write or phone the Yellowstone Park Foundation, 37 East Main Street, Suite 4, Bozeman, Montana 59715; 406-586-6303. See the Foundation's website at http://www.ypf.org.

Founded in 1983, the **Greater Yellowstone Coalition** is an advocacy organization that works to preserve and protect the Greater Yellowstone Ecosystem and the quality of life it sustains. To add your voice, contact the Greater Yellowstone Coalition, P.O. Box 1874, Bozeman, Montana 59771; 406-586-1593. On the World Wide Web: http://www.greateryellowstone.org.

Yellowstone National Park was founded on democratic principles. It is our responsibility to assert our democratic rights by speaking out on issues that concern us. The future of the park and of the Greater Yellowstone Ecosystem depends on wise decision making. Get informed and get involved. Take a class, join one of the above organizations, contribute what you can, and communicate with the members of Congress who represent you.

Use what you have learned about Yellowstone to make a difference. Remember: in the cycle of life, everything affects everything else.

BIBLIOGRAPHY

Barber, John F. *Old Yellowstone Views.* Missoula, Mont.: Mountain Press Publishing Company, 1987.

Billings Gazette Staff. *Yellowstone on Fire!* Billings, Mont.: The Billings Gazette, 1989.

Chittenden, Hiram M. *The Yellowstone National Park.* St. Paul: J.E. Haynes, 1927.

Cottrell, William H. *Born of Fire: The Volcanic Origin of Yellowstone National Park.* Boulder, Colo.: Roberts Rinehart, 1987.

Despain, Don G. *Yellowstone Vegetation.* Boulder, Colo.: Roberts Rinehart, 1990.

Federal Writers Project. *Wyoming: A Guide to Its History, Highways, and People.* Reprint of 1941 edition. Lincoln: University of Nebraska Press, 1981.

Henry, Jeff. *Yellowstone Winter Guide.* Niwot, Colo.: Roberts Rinehart, 1993.

Lageson, David R., and Darwin R. Spearing. *Roadside Geology of Wyoming.* Missoula, Mont.: Mountain Press Publishing Company, 1988.

Marschall, Mark C. *Yellowstone Trails: A Hiking Guide.* Yellowstone National Park, Wyo.: The Yellowstone Association, 1990.

McEneaney, Terry. *Birds of Yellowstone.* Boulder, Colo.: Roberts Rinehart, 1988.

McIntyre, Rick. *A Society of Wolves: National Parks and the Battle Over the Wolf.* Stillwater, Minn.: Voyageur Press, 1993.

Morrison, Micah. *Fire in Paradise.* New York: HarperCollins, 1993.

Patent, Dorothy. *Yellowstone Fires: Flames and Rebirth.* New York: Holiday House, 1990.

Peterson, Roger Tory. *A Field Guide to Western Birds.* The Peterson Field Guide Series. Boston: Houghton Mifflin Company, 1990.

Randall, L.R. "Gay." *Footprints Along the Yellowstone.* San Antonio: The Naylor Company, 1961.

Reynolds, Jane, Phil Gates, and Gaden Robinson. *365 Days of Nature and Discovery.* New York: Harry N. Abrams, 1994.

Russell, Osborne. *Journal of a Trapper.* Edited by Aubrey L. Haines. Lincoln: University of Nebraska Press, 1955.

Scieszka, Jon. *The True Story of the Three Little Pigs.* New York: Viking Press, 1989.

Schullery, Paul. *Old Yellowstone Days.* Boulder, Colo: Associated University Press, 1979.

Thomasma, Kenneth. *Moho Wat: Sheepeater Boy Attempts a Rescue.* Jackson, Wyo.: Grandview Publishing Company, 1996.

_____. *Soun Tetoken: Nez Perce Boy.* Grand Rapids, Mich.: Baker Book House, 1984.

Weide, Bruce, and Patricia Tucker. *There's a Wolf in the Classroom!* Minneapolis: Carolrhoda Books, 1995.

White, E. B. *The Trumpet of the Swan.* New York: HarperCollins Children's Books, 1970.

Whittlesey, Lee H. *Death in Yellowstone.* Boulder, Colo.: Roberts Rinehart, 1995.

_____. *Yellowstone Place Names.* Helena, Mont.: Montana Historical Society Press, 1988.

Yellowstone National Park Division of Interpretation. *Ranger Naturalist Manual, Vols. I-III.* Yellowstone National Park, Wyo.: National Park Service, 1997.

INDEX

ABOUT THE AUTHOR

Author Robin Tawney and her daughter Whitney. WILLIAM NICHOLS PHOTO

A journalism graduate of the University of Montana, Robin also is the author of *Young People's Guide to Yellowstone National Park* (Stoneydale Press, 1985) and *Hiking With Kids* (Falcon, 2000). Her articles about conservation have appeared in many publications including *Living Wilderness, Montana Magazine, High Country News,* the *Denver Post,* and *Western Wildlands.* Committed to conservation stewardship and education, Robin serves on the boards of the Cinnabar Foundation and the Montana Natural History Center. In 1976 Robin and her late husband Phil received the American Motors Conservation Award for their conservation work. Robin was honored in 2000 with the Don Aldrich Fish, Wildlife and Conservation Award for her dedication to conservation advocacy and education.

Robin lives in a forested canyon on the outskirts of Missoula, Montana, with her husband William Nichols, daughter Whitney, one dog, two horses, two llamas, and an occasional pet spider.